DIRECT
FROM NATURE

THE OIL SKETCHES
OF THOMAS HILL

June 10th 1873.

P. Bandugeas.

DIRECT FROM NATURE

THE OIL SKETCHES OF THOMAS HILL

by Janice T. Driesbach
with an essay by William H. Gerdts

YOSEMITE ASSOCIATION
YOSEMITE NATIONAL PARK, CALIFORNIA

in association with the
CROCKER ART MUSEUM
SACRAMENTO, CALIFORNIA

Yosemite Association
P.O. Box 545
Yosemite National Park, California 95389

The Yosemite Association is a non-profit,
membership organization dedicated to the
support of Yosemite National Park. Our
publishing program is designed to provide
an educational service and to increase the
public's understanding of Yosemite's special
qualities and needs. To learn more about
our activities and other publications, or for
information about membership, please write
to the above address, or call (209) 379-2646.

The Crocker Art Museum was founded in
1885 and is the oldest public art museum
west of the Mississippi River. As a division
of the Department of Community and
Visitor Services of the City of Sacramento,
the Crocker provides extensive visual arts
exhibitions and educational programs for
the citizens of the region. For further information, please write to the address below,
or call (916) 264-5423.

Crocker Art Museum
216 "O" Street
Sacramento, California 95814

An exhibition entitled *Direct from Nature:
The Oil Sketches of Thomas Hill* was
mounted at the Crocker Art Museum from
January 24 to March 9, 1997. For information on other venues and a list of lenders to
the exhibition, see page 126.

Printed in Hong Kong

Library of Congress Cataloging-in-Publication Data

Driesbach, Janice Tolhurst.
    Direct from nature : the oil sketches of Thomas Hill / by Janice
T. Driesbach ; with an essay by William H. Gerdts.
        p.   cm.
    Exhibition: Crocker Art Museum, Jan 24.–Mar. 9, 1997.
    Includes bibliographical references.
    Includes index.
    ISBN 0-939666-84-7
    1. Hill, Thomas, 1829–   —Exhibitions. 2. Hill, Thomas, 1829–
—Criticism and interpretation. 3. United States in art—
Exhibitions.   I. Gerdts, William H.   II. Hill, Thomas, 1829–
III. Crocker Art Museum.   IV. Title.
ND237.H615A4   1997   96-47648
759.13—dc21   CIP

FRONTISPIECE:
Thomas Hill, photographed about 1875.
Crocker Art Museum.

TITLE PAGE:
Peter Baumgras
(1827–1903)
*Three Artists Sketching (Juan B.
Wandesforde, Thomas Hill, and
William Marple)*, 1873.
Graphite on paper, 8½ x 10¾ in.
California Historical Society, San Francisco.

CONTENTS PAGE:
Thomas Hill
Crescent Lake, Yosemite, n.d.
Oil on paper, 14 x 21 in.
Kenneth Householder.

Contents

FOREWORD

Created in the field, directly from nature, Thomas Hill's oil sketches are a record of a nineteenth-century artist's delight in the natural world. One of California's finest landscape painters, Hill is known for his large canvases of Yosemite Valley, which he produced in great number. However, he also created wonderful small paintings on canvas, paper, and board. These "oil sketches" depict a wide range of subjects, including scenes of the White Mountains, Newport, the Pacific Northwest, and Yellowstone, as well as views throughout California. They show the artist's ability to quickly render his motifs, producing complete paintings that can stand on their own. Despite the intrinsic appeal of the locations that these paintings document, and Hill's obvious talent with a brush, these works are not well known. He received little of the fame accorded to two of his contemporaries, Albert Bierstadt and Thomas Moran, for their production of such smaller oil paintings.

The Crocker Art Museum holds an outstanding collection of early California paintings, including several by Thomas Hill. One of the highlights is Hill's *Great Cañon of the Sierra, Yosemite,* 1871, arguably his finest surviving large-scale depiction of the Yosemite area. The Crocker's collection also includes two delightful examples of Hill's oil sketches. The strength of these smaller paintings inspired Crocker curator Janice Driesbach to search for more of Hill's oil sketches and to undertake a study of their role in his art.

Through the exhibition and this publication, we are delighted to share a stunning collection of Thomas Hill's oil sketches, along with new information about the artist and the context in which he worked. It is particularly rewarding to be able to share these treasures with museum audiences on both coasts, and to bring new attention to landscape painting in California.

I would like to recognize Curator of Art Janice Driesbach, not only for her work on Hill's oil sketches published here, but also for her overall guidance of this project. She and other members of the Crocker Art Museum staff, including Registrar Paulette Hennum, Curatorial Assistant Karen Martin, and Curator of Education K. D. Kurutz, skillfully managed the many details required of a major loan exhibition and extensive public programs.

We are grateful to the Yosemite Association and its president, Steven P. Medley, for undertaking this publication. We have enjoyed the collaboration. We offer our thanks also to William Gerdts for contributing his essay about the oil sketch in nineteenth-century American painting. Finally, we are indebted to the many individuals and institutions who have lent to the exhibition and who have agreed to have their works reproduced here. Through their generosity, others will delight in Thomas Hill's splendid oil sketches.

Stephen C. McGough
Director
Crocker Art Museum

ACKNOWLEDGMENTS

Direct from Nature: The Oil Sketches of Thomas Hill was made possible by the assistance of many people who generously contributed to both the exhibition and publication. The enthusiasm and understanding of John Garzoli, owner of the Garzoli Gallery and compiler of outstanding documentation of Hill's paintings, have been particularly important. His unsparing assistance to this project is greatly appreciated. Both he and Alfred C. Harrison, Jr., director of the North Point Gallery and an early California art scholar, assisted me in locating Hill oil sketches and encouraged loans to the exhibition. Mr. Harrison and Dr. Oscar Lemer, who also has conducted in-depth research on artists working in Yosemite, generously provided me with contemporary newspaper clippings and shared their knowledge of Hill's development.

Nan and Roy Farrington Jones conferred with me and graciously showed me images of Hill's small paintings from their comprehensive early California art slide archive, and Jan Capecci and Harvey Jones at the Oakland Museum of California allowed valuable access to archives and other resources. Dave Forgang and Linda Eade aided my research at the Yosemite National Park Research Library.

Steve Medley, the staff of the Yosemite Association, and designer Sandy Bell gave generously of their time and talents in creating this publication.

In addition, I am grateful to Nancy K. Anderson of the National Gallery of Art, Katherine Church Holland and Michael McCone at The California

Historical Society, Col. Merl M. Moore, Jr., Dr. Thomas Rogers, Shirley Sargent, Charles Vogel, and many others who assisted by providing information on both Thomas Hill and the sites depicted in both his large and small works.

I would like to express deep appreciation to all those who shared paintings from their collections for inclusion in the exhibition and book. Many of Thomas Hill's finest oil sketches are owned by private collectors, and their thoughtfulness will allow thousands of people to discover, learn about, and enjoy these remarkable paintings.

Finally, generous support by the law firm of Orrick, Herrington and Sutcliffe LLP and a donation from Michael and Leslie Schroeder have contributed significantly to the Crocker Art Museum's ability to present the *Direct from Nature* exhibition and its accompanying programs.

I am confident that, thanks to the contributions of so many, this project will engender greater understanding of Hill and his accomplishments, and that increased enthusiasm will be generated for landscape painting in America during the last half of the nineteenth century.

Janice T. Driesbach
Curator
Crocker Art Museum

DIRECT FROM NATURE
The Oil Sketches of Thomas Hill

JANICE T. DRIESBACH

Thomas Hill
(United States, 1829–1908)
Artist at his Easel in the Woods, n.d.
Oil on paper mounted on panel, 21 x 13¾ in.
Courtesy of Kral Fine Arts, Oakland,
California.

THE WORK OF NINETEENTH-CENTURY landscape painter Thomas Hill (1829–1908) is relatively little-known today, meriting only brief mention in standard American art history texts.[1] But in his time, Hill earned favorable comparison with Albert Bierstadt in the East Coast press (on his return to the United States from Europe in 1867), and received highest honors for landscape painting (at the Philadelphia Centennial). By the early 1870s, his monumental canvases of Yosemite commanded five thousand dollars apiece and attracted national critical acclaim. This recognition afforded Hill a leading role among California artists while San Francisco was becoming established as a major American art center. His residency there brought credibility and attention to Northern California artists as they developed their skills and reputations.

Hill is generally associated with large Yosemite paintings or his *The Driving of the Last Spike* (see page 65), the latter being known as much for the artist's fruitless efforts to secure its purchase by Leland Stanford as for its aesthetic merits. These large-scale compositions, which often may have been motivated to appeal to collectors when he was launching his career or combatting declining sales, incompletely represent Thomas Hill's talents and enthusiasms.

Some of the artist's finest achievements are realized in smaller paintings of subjects as diverse as Newport, Rhode Island, the White Mountains, Mount Shasta and Lake Tahoe in California, and the Pacific Northwest. These modest paintings eloquently attest to Hill's powers of observation, his abilities to render immediate descriptions of his subjects, and his enchantment with his motifs. While *plein air* (outdoor, directly from the landscape) painting had been popular with American artists since the 1840s, Hill was a leader in strongly encouraging critics and collectors in San Francisco to recognize these small-scale paintings as independent works of art.

Oil sketches—here defined as paintings measuring under sixteen-by-twenty inches and generally made on paper or board—comprised a significant portion of Thomas Hill's work from at least the early 1870s. Often highly developed, they range from broadly rendered notations to more detailed presentations. Hill apparently created oil sketches alongside and in nearly equal quantity to his larger paintings for several decades, as documented by

contemporary newspaper descriptions, account books the artist maintained, and sales catalogues.[2]

Even though many of Hill's paintings have been lost to the vicissitudes of time, including devastating fires in California where many of his collectors resided, over 250 oil sketches survive, suggesting Hill's abundant production and their importance to him.[3] Many are signed, indicating that Hill regarded the pieces as independent, fully-realized compositions rather than as working studies. Some of Hill's oil sketches were made for illustrations in other media, notably for reproduction as photogravures and etchings for *Picturesque California* (1888) [figs. 1, 2], and others were sources for larger compositions.

At the same time, many of Hill's small paintings differ distinctly in concept and detail from his larger interpretations of similar subjects on canvas. Spontaneously executed, they capture the artist's direct responses to nature. Whatever their original purposes, and they were undoubtedly multiple, Hill's oil sketches as a body offer immediacy and visual delight, as well as insights into the artist's broad interests and the cultural context in which he worked. And because they represent, in many cases, the only surviving evidence of larger-scale paintings made from them, the oil sketches are key to documenting Hill's career.

YOUTH AND EARLY TRAINING

Born in Birmingham, England, in 1829, Thomas Hill was a contemporary of Frederic Church and Albert Bierstadt. The son of a struggling tailor, however, he was without access to early support for a painting career. After following his father to the United States with his family in 1844, Hill worked briefly in a cotton factory. Fortunately, within a year he obtained an apprenticeship to a carriage painter, which must have offered a welcome alternative to the dreary factory labor. This apprenticeship probably afforded Hill his first (if rudimentary) training in the craft of painting. His employer's assistance in securing him a position with an interior decoration firm in Boston by 1847 suggests that Hill displayed diligence and talent.[4]

Little documentation exists about Thomas Hill's activities during the late 1840s. At some time during this period he may have become acquainted with the painter Virgil Williams (fig. 3), who lived in Taunton, Massachusetts.[5] It is likely that Hill's primary concerns were meeting his expenses and contributing to his family's income, and that much of the youth's energies were consumed by his employment as a decorative painter. Whether Hill sought additional painting lessons at this time, or ventured outside Boston to sketch nearby landscapes is not known.

By the end of 1851, when he was twenty-two, Hill had married Charlotte Hawkes and fathered a son, Edward Rufus. According to family records, twins who died in infancy also arrived, although their birth dates are not noted.[6] Despite the growing size and requirements of his family, Hill resolved to pursue formal art studies and moved to Philadelphia in 1853. Perhaps inspired by Williams's decision to travel to Italy to study art that year, Hill is credited with enrolling in night classes overseen by Peter Rothermel at the Pennsylvania Academy of Fine Arts.[7] The challenges of beginning formal studies at the rather advanced age of twenty-four must have been daunting to Hill. Why he left Boston to study in Pennsylvania, and what Rothermel, an academic painter best known for historical narrative compositions (fig. 4), may have offered him, are intriguing questions.

As an entering student in an informal program, Hill probably had limited contact with Rothermel. His assignments likely would have consisted chiefly of drawing antique casts, with the senior artist periodically critiquing his student's progress.[8] Rothermel's influence might be apparent in Hill's early painting of the *Merchant of Venice* (1865), but that painting has not been located. Alas, almost no evidence of the Hill association with Rothermel survives.

Hill's activities during the ensuing years are also sparsely recorded. He must have been encouraged by the silver medal he earned for a still life exhibited at the Maryland Institute in 1853, and the offer of membership in the Graphic Club.[9] Reportedly, as early as the summer of 1854, he began visiting the White Mountains, where he became friends with Benjamin Champney and painted with other artists associated with the Hudson River School.[10] The following year Hill apparently returned to Massachusetts, and in 1856 he was listed as a resident of Chelsea in the *Boston Business Directory,* with a studio at Assembly Hall.

In 1858 Hill exhibited thirty oil paintings described as "carefully finished from sketches" at Leonard and Company in Boston. This is the first indication that Hill prepared paintings in the studio from studies, and they were judged as "pleasing compositions for the drawing room or parlor."[11] Otherwise his work attracted little notice, which, with the addition of three more children to the Hill family between 1857 and 1860, may have prompted the artist's return to employment as a furniture decorator in 1859.

Hill undoubtedly kept abreast of local art news at this time. If so, he knew of the success Albert Bierstadt encountered upon arriving in New Bedford from Europe the previous year. Word of Bierstadt's first trip west in the summer of 1859, as well as news of his return to the East that fall with numerous sketches, photographs, and Indian artifacts may well have reached Hill. Certainly he would have noted the public attention accorded the exhibition of Bierstadt's *Base of the Rocky Mountains, Laramie Peak* in New York in 1860 and the excitement generated by his treatment of the American West (a subject to which Bierstadt was laying claim).[12]

Now over thirty, Hill must surely have wondered if his own ambitions as an artist would be realized. His growing family and the political uncertainty preceding the outbreak of the Civil War would have caused him apprehension and anxiety. These and other factors may have contributed to the breakdown of Hill's health that is cited as decisive in his departure for California by mid-April, 1861.[13]

ARRIVAL IN SAN FRANCISCO

The details of Hill's relocation to San Francisco are uncertain. Although there is a listing in the 1861 *City Directory* for Hopps, Kanary & Hill (house, sign, and ornamental painters), it is not until an 1862–63 publication that a Thomas Hill, portrait painter lodged at 420 Montgomery Street, is mentioned.[14]

Hill's arrival coincided with an influx of artists into California after the frenzy of the gold rush, but prior to the prosperous years that followed the completion of the transcontinental railroad and the discovery of Comstock Lode silver. At the time of his arrival, the city's premier resident artist, Charles Christian Nahl, was engaged as an illustrator and portrait painter, with the assistance of his compatriot August Wenderoth. Carleton Watkins, active in California as a photographer since 1854, made his first mammoth plate photographs of Yosemite in 1861, and within the year Virgil Williams arrived to work as overseer of the art gallery Robert B. Woodward was establishing in his San Francisco home. Samuel Marsden Brookes, an itinerant portraitist from Wisconsin, also immigrated to San Francisco in 1862, and soon began painting distinguished still lifes (fig. 5).[15]

Hill undoubtedly set himself up as a portraitist, because there was a strong market for that specialty. That he also chose to depict other subjects at this time is exemplified by a painting of the Gould and Curry Company Mill in Virginia City that was exhibited in the window of Jones, Wooll & Sutherland, art suppliers.[16]

Ironically, only days after this piece earned favorable notice, Albert Bierstadt arrived in San Francisco with his illustrious traveling companion, Fitz Hugh Ludlow. The pair, who soon departed for Yosemite Valley with Virgil Williams and Enoch Wood Perry, caused considerable comment among resident artists. Interestingly, one of the next public mentions of Hill, in August 1864, pairs him with the Eastern artist, noting that "T[homas] Hill, another San Francisco artist, offers a cool Sierra Nevada lake scene, with Indians in the foreground and a snow peak in the distance" and referring to "two small Yosemite sketches in oil, by the masterly hand of Bierstadt."[17]

Two months later, the range of Hill's interests was shown in thirteen pieces he submitted to the Mechanics' Institute and Library Industrial Exhibition, one of the few venues for the public display of art work in California at the time. These consisted of six portraits, a "fancy sketch," and six landscapes. Hill seems to have traveled extensively, for the landscapes featured a variety of Northern California scenes, among them Napa Valley, the Russian River, and Soda Springs and Lake Tahoe in the Sierra. Though he probably had not visited Yosemite Valley, there were a number of motivations for him to do so. These included the impressive landscape photographs Carleton Watkins displayed in the same exhibition.[18]

The year 1865 appears to have been pivotal both for Hill and for the arts in San Francisco. In January, the Art Union, an artists' group organized under Brookes's leadership, was founded. Hill lent several paintings to its inaugural exhibition, including views of San Mateo County and Napa Valley. These

FIGURE 5
Samuel Marsden Brookes
(United States, 1816–1892)
Still Life, 1862.
Oil on canvas, 34 x 44 in.
Crocker Art Museum.

were noted in San Francisco newspapers, as were their purchases by local residents.[19] Within two months, Hill contributed a new landscape to the gallery, *Sugar Loaf Peak, El Dorado County* (fig. 6), described as "the boldest and best of his landscapes, and evinc[ing] marked improvement, resulting from that earnest study and conscientious purpose which characterizes the true artist."[20]

While Hill was beginning to attract notice in San Francisco, Bierstadt was using sketches from his California journey to create awesome canvases of Yosemite's grandeur for East Coast audiences. Although met with mixed criticism, his *Looking Down Yosemite Valley, California* (fig. 7) was displayed prominently at the National Academy of Design's Annual Exhibition in 1865. And *Mount Hood, Oregon*, a monumental composition that Bierstadt also exhibited, has been seen as representing "an ambitious attempt to capitalize on new subject matter that Bierstadt rightly perceived would have wide popular appeal."[21] Certainly it generated attention, and Bierstadt's New York reviews were reprinted in San Francisco, with *The Golden Era* repeating the call:

Why should our artists make their pilgrimage to the Alps for mountains, to
Italy for skies, or to the Chamouni Valley, when we have the mountains
and skies of California, and the valley of Yo-Semite. . . . Our young landscape painters should not fail to study and understand the principles upon
which this fine work is painted. It will be of incalculable benefit to them.[22]

SIERRA AND WEST COAST VIEWS

That August, Hill made his first documented visit to Yosemite with Williams
and Watkins (fig. 8). Although their advice on the future of the area had been
requested by Frederick Law Olmsted, Hill's contribution to the ensuing report
is unclear. The *Evening Bulletin* recorded that he and Williams were in
Yosemite and that "when they return we may hope to see some of their latest
studies of that wonderful scenery."[23]

For the opening of the Art Union's second exhibition in October, Hill presented three Yosemite views, the largest of which was praised as "the best general representation of the whole valley we have yet had on canvas."[24] Further, he was awarded the highest honor for his *Merchant of Venice* (which was purchased for six hundred dollars), and reproductions of the work were to be distributed to Art Union members as a benefit.[25] Again following in Bierstadt's footsteps, Hill the next month "completed a painting of Mount Hood . . . which for firmness of outline, depth of color and effective composition, is the best work we have seen from his easel."[26]

By the close of 1865, Hill appears to have significantly extended his familiarity with the prized landmarks of the West Coast, and developed a patronage at the same time. His accomplishments—including sales—were given public notice, and he reportedly held "commissions for several Yosemite scenes." Hill's repertoire of subjects had expanded to include Mount Baker in Oregon, Mount St. Helens, and other views of the Washington Territory. This increased visibility undoubtedly reflected his growing skills and the greater commitment of his time to landscape painting. With his work in some demand, he began to explore additional West Coast themes, either visiting new places or using photographs and paintings by others as models.[27]

The painting *Sugar Loaf Peak, El Dorado County* (fig. 6) offers insights into the artist's development to this time. This work evinces a clarity and even-handed attention to detail that demonstrate Hill's continued practice of idioms from the Hudson River School to which he had been introduced in the East. The composition's cohesiveness engages the viewer, with the Native American figures providing a center of interest that balances the trees and owl in the right foreground.

Byrne's Ferry on the Stanislaus River (fig. 9), which like most of Hill's small paintings is undated, is consistent in technique and style with his accomplishments of the mid-1860s. A motif that probably was recorded on the artist's Yosemite journey, it shares the pastel tones and descriptive detail of Hill's compositions of this period. Even though painted on canvas, *Byrne's Ferry on the Stanislaus River* suggests Hill was making oil sketches by 1865; it also illustrates the artist's propensity for including figures, structures, and incidental details in his outdoors studies.

Not only are the activities of the ferry that transported visitors to Yosemite recorded, but, tellingly, Hill inserted himself in the left foreground with brush in hand, working on what appears to be either paper or a small fragment of unstretched canvas. Harking back to images by Asher B. Durand and other Hudson River School painters, the idyllic scene shows the artist in harmony with the setting, where the human presence, although acknowledged, appears insignificant when compared to the uninhabited wilderness that lies beyond.

As these and other paintings, such as *Emerald Bay, Lake Tahoe* (fig. 10) attest, Hill's abilities were becoming quite substantial. Both his confidence and his pattern of emulating Bierstadt are indicated in Hill's submission of *View of the Yosemite Valley* (fig. 11) to the 1866 National Academy of Design exhibition. Although much more modest than Bierstadt's painting of the previous year,

FIGURE 9
Thomas Hill
Byrne's Ferry on the Stanislaus River, n.d.
Oil on canvas, 12 x 16 in.
The Bancroft Library, University of
California, Berkeley.

FIGURE 10
Thomas Hill
Emerald Bay, Lake Tahoe, 1864.
Oil on canvas, 36 x 56 in.
Los Angeles County Museum of Art,
William Randolph Hearst Collection.

the composition was accepted and must have invited comparison. Bierstadt's achievements undoubtedly underscored Hill's awareness that his training was limited and that opportunities for further study in California were unavailable.

EUROPEAN SOJOURN

A number of other factors coalesced in Hill's world and led him to a new phase in his life at this time. Not only was the American public eager to put the Civil War behind it, but there were optimistic economic prospects. In addition, the Exposition Universelle of 1867, to feature displays of art and technology from thirty-two countries, was slated to open in Paris in April. Hill, ready for a change, ended his first stay in California, most likely in the late spring of 1866. At the beginning of July he applied for his passport in the East, and presumably departed for France shortly thereafter.[28]

Hill's activities during his ten months in Europe are poorly documented. He must have viewed the great display of contemporary international art at the Exposition Universelle near the end of his trip. This event offered American artists a rare opportunity for firsthand exposure to the accomplishments of highly-regarded French and British artists. Contrary to later press accounts, Hill's work was not included in the exhibition, but surely he was aware of the criticisms the American section sustained. Among the Americans, only Church earned a prize (a silver medal for his *Niagara*), and Bierstadt's achievements were passed over, causing much discussion.[29] The condemnation was widespread:

> Few critics discussed questions of style, or mentioned works of higher quality that had been left at home. Rather, despite the preponderance of American subjects in the gallery, most critics objected that the entries from the United States were neither native nor descriptive enough, and insufficiently documented the characteristic aspects of American life. They

pointed to the absence of certain typical American scenes ('there should have been a prairie, a sierra, and some views of New England home life and pioneer life'), and noted that, except for pictures by Church and Bierstadt, few landscapes were distinctly American.[30]

According to published accounts, Hill studied with Paul Meyerheim in Paris. A member of a distinguished family of artists from Danzig, Meyerheim is best known for paintings of animals and genre scenes, and for his prints and illustrations. He traveled throughout Europe, and his early landscape paintings were influenced by contemporary French art.[31] Although Meyerheim reportedly encouraged Hill to focus on landscape painting, Hill was predisposed to this specialty. Further, the fact that critics noted the absence of such work from the American display in Paris would have bolstered his preference for this subject matter.

The key benefit Hill appears to have received from Meyerheim (as well as from other French artists) was firsthand exposure to Barbizon painting. This school offered models for treating his canvases more broadly, employing the use of small brush strokes or even daubs of color to effectively signify foliage and figures. Hill's layering of pigment to achieve foreground richness also may have been inspired by the Barbizon artists. With these new techniques, Hill was better able to enliven his canvases and vary his paint handling. That this allowed him to more effectively unify his compositions and address the imposing vistas offered by such subjects as Yosemite Valley is documented in paintings that followed.

Few paintings undertaken by Hill in France have been identified. Interestingly, there is considerable evidence that he continued to explore California motifs rather than undertake new European subjects. A series of three paintings of Yosemite Valley from 1867 may have been created abroad, judging from the inscription "Paris, 1867" on one of the canvases (fig. 12). This group of paintings, rendered from the valley floor with a focus on the meandering Merced River, shows striking parallels to the photograph *View Up the Valley from the Foot of El Capitan* that Carleton Watkins published in 1863 (fig. 13). Their similarities suggest that Hill either took Watkins's images of Yosemite with him, or had access to them in France. That he used photographs, either alone or in combination with small oil "sketches," as sources for compositions he created then (and throughout his career) is evident.[32]

Why Hill chose to paint Yosemite subjects in Europe is uncertain. The fact that Watkins's Yosemite photographs were awarded a bronze medal at the Exposition Universelle, and that he was achieving international renown for these views, may have influenced the decision. It also seems likely that Hill continued to paint with the interests of American collectors in mind.

PAINTING YOSEMITE IN BOSTON

By late spring of 1867, Hill returned to the United States. At the end of the year he was renting work space at the Studio Building in Boston, and residing in Cambridge.[33] Thereafter he set to work on California views, including his first monumental Yosemite scene. Hill invited press attention, and a *Boston*

FIGURE 12
Thomas Hill
Yosemite Valley, 1867.
Oil on canvas, 15 x 26 in.
Courtesy of Montgomery Gallery,
San Francisco.

FIGURE 13
Carleton Watkins
*View Up the Valley from the Foot of El
Capitan,* 1863.
Albumen silver print, 7⅝ x 11¾ in.
California Historical Society, San Francisco.

Evening Transcript article of February 24, 1868, uses Church's *Niagara* and Bierstadt's *Domes of the Yosemite*, the two most famous paintings of the day, as benchmarks for the unfinished Yosemite composition.[34] When Hill exhibited his *Yosemite Valley* at the Childs & Co. gallery in Boston four months later, the *Boston Post* published a notice of the upcoming event, and an enthusiastic review appeared in the *Evening Transcript*.

In the notice, Bierstadt and "the genius of Starr King" are credited with generating interest in Yosemite in Boston, and the writer observes that "Hill now enters the arena and with a success that will add new interest to the subject and country." A detailed description of the composition followed.[35]

Four days later, a reviewer cited Hill's *Yosemite Valley* as "representing quite literally the sublimist of scenery. . . . It resembles in subject and treatment to some extent Bierstadt's picture; but it is not at all an imitation; neither does it deal with the same prospect."[36] Indeed, Hill's composition differed significantly from Bierstadt's (and his own previous) representations of Yosemite in its dramatic view from Inspiration Point above the valley. In selecting this site for his painting, Hill offered a new interpretation of a locale that was rapidly becoming familiar to Eastern audiences.

These comments (by unidentified authors) on Hill's work suggest that besides artistic proficiency, the artist developed new public relations skills in Europe. The articles include otherwise unsubstantiated comments on the enthusiastic reception of Hill's work at the Exposition Universelle (in which he was not represented), reports on the lavish praise he received from the eminent French academic painter Thomas Couture, and the pronouncement that *Yosemite Valley* was "composed from sketches taken on the spot; and thus reproduces rather than suggests the grand features of the landscape."[37]

Although such reports of his drawing from oil studies might have been intended to associate Hill with Bierstadt, they may represent just as well an effort to deflect criticism of Hill's more likely practice of basing his monumental compositions on photographs, quite probably those taken by Watkins. If anything, this passage may mislead rather than enlighten readers as to the role oil sketches played in Hill's *oeuvre* at this time.[38]

Though he had been absent from California for nearly two years, Hill created in *Yosemite Valley* a remarkably accurate rendering of many major Yosemite landmarks in a unified composition that conveys the majestic character of the landscape. To create a cohesive image of this imposing subject on a monumental scale would have required reference sources. It was not uncommon to use photography as a tool at this time (or to minimize the role it played). Hill almost certainly drew from Watkins's vision (which had been amply rewarded) to create his composition, as he strived to achieve a distinctive approach to this immensely popular subject.

FIGURE 15
Thomas Hill
Gathering Sedge, ca. 1875.
Oil on paper mounted on board, 14 x 20 ½ in.
Private collection.

Hill's ambition for his *Yosemite Valley* is reflected in his asking price of ten thousand dollars for the painting in Boston. The piece stirred interest, and Louis Prang commissioned a smaller version of the subject to reproduce as a chromolithograph (fig. 14). But there was no mention that *Yosemite Valley* had sold when it was exhibited in San Francisco fourteen months later and was described in the *News Letter* as the most pleasing painting of Yosemite to date. The strongest likelihood is that *Yosemite Valley* was purchased by railroad magnate Charles Crocker in California.[39]

PAINTING IN THE FIELD

Meanwhile, Hill was traveling to various Eastern locations. He reportedly undertook "small canvases, mainly coast views," on order during the summer of 1868. An undated sample of such a subject, *Gathering Sedge* (fig. 15), made at Second Beach in Newport, demonstrates the change in Hill's style following his return from Europe. In contrast to his earlier paintings, broad swatches of paint define the water, beach, and, in the distance, Bishop Berkeley's Rock. Even the foreground figures are effectively defined by dabs of paint, and Hill appears to have quickly rendered his subject. This spot on the Newport coastline was recorded by Worthington Whittredge as early as 1865, and may have come to Hill's attention through contact with his colleague.[40]

Hill made small paintings from nature at Niagara Falls (perhaps inspired by Church), Goodrich Falls, and the White Mountains, returning from New Hampshire with some fifty sketches, in his new style, that he intended to draw upon for larger canvases. His direct treatment of his motifs likely found an appreciative audience in Boston, where Barbizon School painting was enthusiastically collected. By this time his oil studies were becoming central to Hill's work, and he was perceived in the East as one of its most promising landscape painters.[41]

During a fall 1868 visit to Whittier's birthplace in East Haverhill, Massachusetts, Charles Brainard wrote of Hill's skill at quickly sketching his subjects. Leaving Hill at his easel, Brainard ambled to the house, and upon

> returning to the brook-side where I had left the artist at work, I found him surrounded by a group of men and boys, who looked with intent and evident delight at an admirable sketch in oil colors of the house and barn, and the picturesque scenery.[42]

This sketch, which has been documented but is unlocated, apparently served as a model for a larger painting (fig. 16) whose accuracy Whittier praised, and also was published as a chromolithograph by Prang (one of four additional prints the publisher made from Hill's paintings around 1870).[43]

By 1869 Hill was therefore making oil sketches both for reproduction (perhaps initially suggested by Prang) and as studies—witness *Profile Peak from Profile Lake, New Hampshire* (fig. 17). That composition is closely replicated in a larger painting, and testifies to Hill's practice of using single oil sketches from nature rather than combining several sketches for his larger works.

His summer tour to the White Mountains, an enormously popular sketching spot for artists—including Bierstadt—during the 1860s, yielded a view of Franconia Notch with Echo Lake that drew press attention. Indeed, Hill's New England scenes elicited appreciation for the range of abilities they represented. His talents for depicting Yosemite's sublime vistas already recognized, Hill was acknowledged for responding to subjects "nearer our knowledge, and can paint a sylvan scene, by which an ordinary mind would pass entirely unobservant," such as Lake Kinos, made famous by Whittier.[44]

FIGURE 16
Thomas Hill
Birthplace of John Greenleaf Whittier, 1868.
Oil on canvas, 30 x 46½ in.
Haverhill Public Library, Massachusetts.

Hill's skill at rapidly creating small paintings in the field was also documented by his friend Champney, who commented that "Thomas Hill has all the facility of Bierstadt, and can make more pictures in a given time than any man I ever met. In one afternoon of three hours in the White Mountain forests I have seen him produce a study, 12 x 20 in size, full of details and brilliant light. There is his greatest strength, and his White Mountain wood studies have not been excelled."[45]

FIGURE 17
Thomas Hill
Profile Peak from Profile Lake, New Hampshire, 1869.
Oil on paper mounted on board, 13 x 19 in.
Garzoli Gallery, San Rafael, California.

Surely some of Hill's small paintings required many hours to complete. Others exhibit more summary execution, and confirm that the artist achieved consummate skill at quickly rendering landscape views. In his haste, Hill often painted into wet pigment and used only touches of oil to signify a head or foliage. The success of the resulting images, which complemented larger oils on canvas, is indicated by the contemporary judgment that "Mr. Hill has given us prose and poetry with the same inspired pencil."[46]

Besides exhibiting his monumental *Yosemite Valley* at Snow and Roos in San Francisco, Hill regularly sent paintings to California from Boston. This activity and the artist's continued use of California landscape themes fueled speculation he would soon return to the Pacific Coast "to obtain fresh sketches of scenery."[47] Prior to late 1871, however, Hill probably confined his travels to New England, with one or more tours to Niagara Falls.

CRITICAL ACCLAIM IN THE EAST

Despite accounts to the contrary, Hill's activities in early 1871 indicate that he was prepared to settle in the East. His large painting entitled *White Mountain Notch* was a critical and popular success when shown at Childs & Co. in December 1870. According to local papers, the composition (previously shown in both Philadelphia and New York) attracted a large number of viewers and was called by many "the finest piece of New England landscape scenery ever exhibited in Boston." Basking in this praise and poised to undertake a number of commissions, Hill built a new studio in Cambridge, which he occupied by January.[48]

Although Edward Bosqui later recalled the artist's presence at the founding meeting of the San Francisco Art Association that spring, Hill is not recorded as attending any of the organization's meetings until late in 1871. It is not likely that Hill was one of the originators, for, in citing the need for such a group, the *San Francisco News Letter* referred to Hill as "the pet of Boston," and listed other artists who had left California to achieve success in Europe or the East.[49]

His friend Virgil Williams returned to California in mid-1871 (as did Bierstadt), but Hill does not seem to have traveled west that summer. Indeed, the Art Association minutes of November 2 listing him in attendance and his exhibition of "study pictures" of Yosemite scenes at the Boston Art Club in December offer the sole evidence of such a journey, which must have been brief.[50]

FIGURE 19
Thomas Hill
Great Cañon of the Sierra, Yosemite, 1871.
Oil on canvas, 72 x 120 in.
Crocker Art Museum.

FIGURE 20
Carleton Watkins
The Yosemite Valley from Inspiration Point on the Mariposa Trail, 1863.
Albumen silver print, 7⅝ x 11¾ in.
California Historical Society, San Francisco.

For by November 18, Hill was exhibiting his second monumental view of Yosemite, *Great Cañon of the Sierra, Yosemite* (fig. 19), in his Boston studio. The six-by-ten-foot canvas, also from a viewpoint overlooking the valley but "some five miles" from the vantage of his earlier painting, must have occupied him for some time. On its public showing, the *Boston Evening Transcript* weighed in on the artist's behalf, pronouncing it "a success, and the grandest one Mr. Hill has achieved."[51]

The enthusiasm that greeted the *Great Cañon of the Sierra, Yosemite* in the Boston press paled in comparison to the response generated when the painting traveled to New York in January 1872. When the work was exhibited at the Palette Club late that month, *Watson's Art Journal* declared it a national as well as a personal success, opening its review by saying:

> If it be true that Art, like Christianity and Civilization, has for its mission to bring us back to Nature and so to God,—then indeed is Thomas Hill. . . the apostle of Truth, in whose capacious brain the majestic forms and subtle effects of Nature have come to rest; and in the 'Canyon of the Sierras' he has given us the incarnation of his ideas, with all the power, freshness and grandeur of nature.
>
> From a national point of view we look upon this as a representative picture, and one that not only the Palette Club but all Americans can be proud of.[52]

Two months later, the same publication disparaged Albert Bierstadt's *In the Rocky Mountains,* with the comment that

> Mr. Bierstadt's imagination is beyond his powers of execution and . . . he generally fails to give a satisfactory and perfect picture through attempting too much. . . . In this respect he compares unfavorably with his rival, and, we think, superior, Thomas Hill, who possesses a freshness, originality, and power which nothing of Mr. Bierstadt's, that we have seen, can equal.[53]

RETURN TO CALIFORNIA

Although Hill must have savored this critique, he was facing challenges in the East. A financial crisis in New York in 1869 affected art patronage, and Hill's health was suffering.[54] By early May, he had reappeared in California on a visit to Mount St. Helena, where he camped out and sketched with his friend and fellow artist, Virgil Williams."[55]

As Hill had been regularly recording views firsthand from nature following his return to the United States, it is no surprise that he and Williams painted outdoors together during the trip. Scenes such as *Our Camp* (fig. 21), in which the white canvas tent and awning are foils for cooking implements and tin cans, and *Virgil Williams' Cabin near Saint Helena* (fig. 22) speak to the friendship and intimacy the artists shared.

Another impetus for Hill's trip West may have been his need to oversee the exhibition of *Great Cañon of the Sierra, Yosemite* in San Francisco in late May. Its presentation under gaslight in a substantial walnut frame manufactured by Snow and Roos, with the gallery otherwise darkened, paralleled the theatrical settings in which Bierstadt's early Rocky Mountain and Yosemite scenes were shown.[56]

The painting's reception in San Francisco was enthusiastic, with one reviewer pronouncing it "the grandest picture ever exhibited in this State." A lengthy description in the *Evening Bulletin* noted that although it was painted in Boston, *Great Cañon of the Sierra, Yosemite* "has been retouched and completed since its arrival here, nearly the whole foreground having been painted over." The account then contrasted the sunlit view with the atmospheric effects of Hill's earlier Yosemite painting in Charles Crocker's collection.[57]

Saliently, the same article credited California collectors for the taste they demonstrated in purchasing both of Hill's monumental Yosemite paintings. Even before it was placed on exhibition at Snow and Roos, *Great Cañon of the Sierra, Yosemite* had been acquired by E. B. Crocker for a reported $10,000 to add to the growing collection of California art in the new gallery adjoining his Sacramento home. That Hill's second monumental Yosemite canvas also was bought by a California business leader testifies to the popularity of Yosemite subjects in San Francisco, and illustrates the importance of the California art market to Hill's livelihood at this time.[58]

Given Hill's preparations to exhibit Eastern scenes, making "wood and mountain studies," and his start on a painting of the Golden Gate, it appears that his health had steadied by June of 1872. He reportedly visited Massachusetts in August, and returned to San Francisco with his family the next month. There was increased demand for his work in San Francisco, and as its art community began to thrive, Hill's hard-won professional stature made him a lead-

FIGURE 23
Thomas Hill
Mount St. Helena, Napa Valley, n.d.
Oil on paper mounted on board,
13¾ x 20¾ in.
Private collection, courtesy of Garzoli Gallery,
San Rafael, California.

ing painter there.[59] Despite his prominence in California, however, Hill was challenged to maintain a national reputation while working across the continent from Eastern art centers.

By November, Hill had opened a studio in San Francisco, exhibiting, among others, scenes of Mount St. Helena. These offerings, described as "admirable studies," were most likely oil sketches Hill had made with Williams the previous spring, and may have included compositions such as *Mount St. Helena, Napa Valley* (fig. 23). This work effectively captures the fleeting fog that shrouds the tree tops in the middle distance.

CALIFORNIA SKETCH TRIPS

The importance that sketching in the field had assumed for the artist is indicated by the fact that he had "lately been out on another sketching trip," and that in the ensuing weeks, his small paintings garnered a number of favorable comments. His contribution of a "beautiful sketch of Yosemite Valley" to an auction benefiting the family of fellow artist Fortunato Arriola was noted.[60] And a reviewer of Hill's entry in the San Francisco Art Association exhibition in December called it

> a beautiful little bit, a man fishing—trouting—standing just in the light of a *vista* through the trees, the foliage of which is made with that effect that means something with every touch, almost legerdemain of manipulation, acquired by study and work.[61]

The activity of fishing is the subject of some of Hill's finest oil sketches. Dating primarily to the 1870s, scenes of fishermen alone and in small parties by streams and in boats, rank among the artist's most satisfying efforts. The oil sketch format is ideally suited to the intimacy of the theme, and the interplay of light and shadow inherent in the subject allowed Hill to display his facility for capturing such effects. Scenes such as *The Angler* (fig. 24) and *Thomas Hill and Virgil Williams with Their Wives Fishing* (fig. 25) show faces and foliage rendered with a dash or stroke of paint, and use color effectively to tie the compositions together.

These unpretentious subjects depict quiet moments of individual or shared enjoyment, the recording of which must have brought the artist much pleasure. In the simple recreations they register, their rural settings, and their

execution out-of-doors, they are reminiscent of the early impressionist paintings Monet and Renoir created at LaGrenouillère at about the same time.

In early 1873, Hill participated in exhibitions at the Atheneum in Boston (where he was a member of the Art Club) and in San Francisco. In California, his recently completed six-by-ten-foot painting *The Royal Arches of Yosemite* was displayed on loan from William Ralston, another eminent San Francisco businessman and art collector.[62] Although this work generated press discussion, it is unclear whether Hill developed the composition from on-site sketches or from other sources. His activities were closely followed in the press, but there is no record that he had revisited Yosemite since his return to California. Newspapers on both coasts carried accounts of Hill, with the *Boston Evening Transcript* expressing renewed concern for the artist's health in February.[63]

In contrast, the San Francisco press made no mention of Hill's health. Rather, a *California Art Gallery* article the following month justified purchases of European art by San Francisco collectors in light of the dearth of local talent, and identified Hill as one of the city's promising painters. That he was being compared favorably to the European artists is indicated in the comment that

Hill, after an association with the best artists and labors of the French and German schools, and after stopping at Boston long enough to practice what Europe taught him, has come here panoplied so royally, that we who knew him in the years gone, among his portraits, scarcely recognize him now. These, and all other artists of worth, are and will continue to be encouraged as they ripen into superiority.[64]

As his exhibition-sized paintings garnered praise, Hill continued to make oil sketches and use them for his work. A river view and a scene of a boy with sheep exhibited at Snow and Roos in April were reportedly "the result of [the artist's] studies in and about the Sonoma Valley." In contrast to Bierstadt and other artists who routinely compiled larger, "fictional" compositions from numbers of oil studies, Hill's large landscapes generally showed actual views, most likely drawn from single studies or a few related sketches. His authenticity was noted in the judgment that "the artist has preserved the character of the country and its flora to the extent that no one who has visited Napa and Sonoma Valleys can fail to recognize the scene."[65]

In the meantime, Hill completed another major exhibition painting called *Home of the Eagle*. Lauded for its "sturdy vigor and good painting," it featured the unusual subject of a large predatory bird about to consume its prey. In commenting on the challenging theme, one critic noted that "the landscape is a composition from a number of out-of-door studies; the eagle is from life."[66]

FIGURE 28
Thomas Hill
Frenchmen's Gulch, n.d.
Oil on paper mounted on board, 15 x 22 in.
Mr. and Mrs. Garrett Plant Scales.

ENTHUSIASM FOR OIL SKETCHES

It was, however, the smaller pictures that Hill had on view with *Home of the Eagle* that prompted one commentator to refer to Hill's claim to a place in the front rank of American artists:

> In . . ."A Forest Scene," for instance, although it is scarcely a foot square, we have a charming bit of woods, with an opening of tender sky. This is all (except the figures of a man and dog) touched in with the nice character and effect which Mr. Hill always gives to his sparingly introduced figures, yet it is painted with such beauty of touch and tone, with so much feeling for nature, and so much truth in the treatment of the trees, that the picture is a gem.[67]

Hill's practice of making small paintings outdoors was not unusual among California artists at the time. The good use Bierstadt made of oil sketches was well known, and the hospitable climate and impressive topographic features of the state would have encouraged this endeavor. In April 1873, *The California Art Gallery* noted that

> Our landscape painters are making preparations for their annual summer sketching tours and will soon be in the field. Bierstadt goes south, where he will make studies of coast scenery, after which he will visit Oregon and sketch along the Columbia River. . . . Hill purposes renewing his acquaintance with the neighborhood of Mount St. Helena, which furnishes a great number of excellent rock and foliage studies.

That summer, however, Hill was, in fact, in the Sierra with William Marple and Hiram Bloomer. Other notable artists on sketching tours included William Keith at Yosemite, Gideon Jacques Denny in Mendocino, and Gilbert Munger "among the lakes of the Sierra."[68]

Hill's oil sketches continued to capture attention, and in late 1873 and 1874, the *News Letter* issued a series of calls for the local Art Association to consider hosting sketch exhibitions. One writer noted that

> many artists' sketches are infinitely better than their finished pictures, and, anyhow, there is a special charm about their fresh out-of-doors studies which all who know anything of art are sure to appreciate. Then, again, many artists make a score or more of sketches to every picture they paint, and it is often very interesting to inspect these preliminary foreshadowings, more especially when the completed work is something out of the common.[69]

Bierstadt, who had recently returned to San Francisco laden with oil sketches of Hetch Hetchy Valley, was credited with inspiring these thoughts. As Bierstadt's extended tour of California was nearing a close, his continued influence as "the foremost landscape artist of America" was reflected in this petition for official acknowledgment of the importance and quality of oil sketches.[70]

When the request was renewed the next month, however, its motivation was Hill's return to San Francisco with over seventy oil sketches of locales such as Donner Lake and Mount Lyell, as well as views of Yosemite from new points. "As regards Mr. Hill's oil sketches, which would of themselves form a very interesting little exhibition, we must say that they are crisp and forcible, full of daylight and charming color, and quite finished enough for the appreciation of all but the utterly obtuse in art."[71] With another of the city's leading artists earning such notoriety for his small works on paper, the oil sketch rapidly gained credibility as a serious medium for artists in California.

FROM SKETCHES TO PAINTINGS

As was their custom, San Francisco's artists returned to studios in the city in the fall to complete commissions or prepare for the upcoming Art Association exhibition. For his part, Hill, in possession of fresh sketches of the area, undertook two "upright, round topped views of Yosemite, which will, when finished, adorn the residence of one of our prominent bankers."[72] The paintings, one reportedly from Glacier Point, the other from Indian Canyon, must have been created from oil sketches such as those that once hung in the offices of William Ralston (figs. 31, 32). Although *Artist's Point and Yosemite Falls* is horizontal and from a different viewpoint, it is certainly related to the Ralston commission.

It is uncertain whether Hill made the small paintings on site with his patron in mind or whether Ralston had ordered the larger compositions from studies he saw in Hill's studio. They do confirm that Hill was engaged in recording Yosemite subjects from different perspectives, and that he had become intrigued with the granaries used by the Sierra Miwok to store acorns, the staple of their diet.

Although these acorn granaries captured the attention of other painters and photographers in Yosemite, Hill's *Indian Camp, Yosemite* offers one of

FIGURE 31
Thomas Hill
Artist's Point and Yosemite Falls, ca. 1873.
Oil on paper mounted on board, 13½ x 20½ in.
Dr. and Mrs. Edward H. Boseker.

FIGURE 32
Thomas Hill
Indian Camp, Yosemite, ca. 1873.
Oil on paper mounted on board,
20½ x 13½ in.
Dr. and Mrs. Edward H. Boseker.

their earliest depictions. Hill frequently showed Native American artifacts or figures in his Yosemite scenes. For, in contrast to Bierstadt, whose monumental compositions were often bereft of people or man-made elements, Hill seldom omitted human references from his large paintings, and often included them in smaller works as well. In this case, the granaries and the nearby Miwok village help direct the viewer's attention through the successive vertical lines created by Yosemite Falls and the screen of tall trees. Again Hill uses small touches of paint to create descriptive highlights—here, white spots adorn garments and serve as the nose and feet of the small dog.

Hill also used his sketches for a large Donner Lake scene. Donner Pass, one of the greatest obstacles to the construction of the Central Pacific Railroad and an embodiment of the hardships of overland passage, was the subject of paintings by Bierstadt and William Keith, as well. In developing his composition, Hill created at least one "cabinet size" picture of Donner. This term was used in the nineteenth century to refer to small paintings created in the studio, generally made on canvas (unlike oil sketches).

That there was contemporary concern with such distinctions and their implications is indicated in a reference to Edwin Deakin, who also was working around Lake Tahoe in 1873. The fifty or so oil studies Deakin brought back to San Francisco that year elicited positive comment, including the observation that "the whole are made on Windsor & Newton's oil 'sketch paper' (or rather card), on which more finish is attainable in one painting than on canvas, and there seems to be no reason why it should not be used for cabinet pictures as well as outdoor studies." This surely helped to validate the use of paper and to hasten the acceptance of oil sketches as finished works of art.[73]

Despite its small size, Hill's cabinet painting of Donner Lake was deemed to have "succeeded in representing the grandeur of the scene very successfully. The cool grey of the morning and the tender distance are both admirably rendered."[74] These qualities also characterize his studies of Donner Lake made on paper (fig. 33). Hill's large canvas of Donner Lake shares many affinities with a painting Bierstadt had completed for Collis Huntington and exhibited in San Francisco in January 1873 (fig. 34).

At the same time, their approaches to the same subject are distinctive. Bierstadt gives prominence to a brilliant rising sun (with its concomitant spiritual connotations) by placing the foreground in relative darkness. While this treatment inspires awe, it keeps the viewer at a distance. Hill's bright, evenly lit lake is shown at mid-day, revealing a foreground scattered with boulders and trees that invites the viewer to enter the scene. The compositional closeness of these images may have been requested by the patron or dictated by the challenge of incorporating both the railroad shed and lake into a single view. In either case, Hill, as he forged his career in California, continued to be influenced by Bierstadt's successes.

ART ACTIVITY IN SAN FRANCISCO

In November, 1873, Hill moved into a new studio in Duncan's Building in San Francisco. He had accumulated oil sketches of both the Sierra Nevada and the Coast Range, and with his Donner Lake commission underway, Hill had "no

FIGURE 33
Thomas Hill
Donner Lake, ca. 1874.
Oil on paper mounted on board, 12 x 22 in.
Private collection.

FIGURE 34
Albert Bierstadt
Donner Lake from the Summit, 1873.
Oil on canvas, 72 x 120 in.
The New-York Historical Society.

present intention of deserting the Coast."[75] This comment may have come in response to the recent departures of both Bierstadt and Gilbert Munger for the East. It also reflected concern for the well-being of the local art community when the economy was faltering and the Art Association was about to open an art school. The operation of a teaching facility was key to San Francisco's development as an important art center, but it would require significant financial support (in an adverse economic climate) from community leaders and collectors.

Up to this time, Hill participated in Art Association exhibitions, attended the group's meetings occasionally, and joined the Bohemian Club, but appears to have refrained from more active involvement in local arts organizations. In late 1873, however, he accepted appointment to the Committee on the School of Design of the Art Association, whereupon he oversaw the selection of his longtime friend Virgil Williams as the school's founding director.[76]

At the beginning of 1874, Hill was working on small views of a beach and a country road, as well as the Yosemite scenes for Ralston. Also underway in his studio were *Source of the Saco* (considered the most ambitious landscape in progress in San Francisco at the time), and a White Mountain view. Hill entered the winter exhibition of the Art Association with

a charming and faithful view of Cascade Lake, near Tahoe. The transparency of the green water in this picture, the graceful group of deer at the edge of the lake, the airy perspective of the distant snow peaks, growing rosy in the evening light—are features showing both feeling for nature and great technical skill. Mr. Hill's small view of Lake Tahoe, looking across Emerald Bay [fig. 35], was also a faithful and pleasing picture.[77]

These comments accord with two exquisite surviving oil sketches, whose subjects are tenderly rendered by Hill (although the first reference was more likely to a larger painting). That he chose to be represented by these pictures in a public exhibition may indicate his justifiable fondness for them, as well as an interest in offering fresh subjects to viewers in San Francisco. Indeed, the appeal Cascade Lake and Emerald Bay held for Hill (or his patrons) is documented in oil sketches and paintings he completed over three decades of his career (figs. 10, 35).

Hill's diverse projects met with some success, with a report made in February that his pictures had commanded the best prices of all the paintings sold in a recent auction.[78] He also was singled out when the *News Letter* renewed its effort on behalf of oil sketches the following month. A lengthy article opens with a tribute to English landscape painters, who are described as following nature pretty closely, and one-half of them finish, or nearly finish, their works *on the spot*. . . . We are glad to note among our artists here the same disposition to supply outdoors. This train of thought was induced by seeing Tom Hill at work on a number of his original oil sketches. His studio work is always full of nature, but his sketches, with the little necessary finish, discount it. Mr. Hill has a most interesting and varied series, and when he has got through with and disposed of them—why, he can go off and sketch some more. Some of our landscapists have expressed a determination to spend months this year in the field, and the resolve is a wise one.[79]

Whether other artists were following suit is difficult to assess, but it is clear that Hill, like Bierstadt, was making a large number of oil sketches at this time, and that these played a significant role in his work.

AUCTION OF ARTWORK

Perhaps encouraged by the *News Letter* campaign, Hill announced a sale of his paintings, to include only oil sketches, for April, 1874. In what seems to have been an innovative way of selling work, Hill engaged Newhall's to auction eighty-three paintings, described as "oil sketches from nature, made at intervals during the last six years."[80] A pre-sale article on the event stated:

> we do not exaggerate in saying that there is a freshness, vigor and truth in all that are seldom found, even in the finest compositions. They represent nature as she really appears in all her wayward and varying moods of sunshine and shadow, calm and storm, forest glade and mountain glacier. Studies of this kind, by first-class painters, have always been valued more highly than even their finished works. . . . An opportunity is afforded by this sale, to persons of even moderate means, to obtain first-class pictures, and the reputation of the painter is such, not only on the Pacific Coast but in the East and in Europe, that we have no doubt that the sale will be the success it deserves to be.[81]

Although Hill added several larger paintings on canvas to his offering as the sale neared, a majority of the works remained "simply finished studies from nature, and *not* studio pictures." This telling description was accompanied by the statement that Hill had already accepted commissions that would consume his time "for two years or more." The local press thus promoted Hill's efforts both by lauding his sketches and emphasizing that additional works by the artist would not be on the market for some time.[82] Despite evidence that his paintings were in demand, however, Hill probably arranged the sale to generate needed income, a supposition supported by the *Daily Alta California* statement that "Mr. Hill has a very good reputation in the Eastern States as well as here, but a short time has elapsed since he began to paint well, and fame has not yet done him justice."[83]

Not surprisingly, Hill's sale was deemed a success by the press. There was speculation that more than half of the paintings were spoken for when the event commenced, and a total of $14,000 was realized in all. Millionaire financiers William Ralston, William Sharon, D. O. Mills, and Leland Stanford

were among the successful bidders, a clear tribute to Hill's high standing among San Francisco's business leaders.

Although one "smaller painting" reportedly fetched $380, the overall average of $165 per painting was considerably lower than the prices Hill had received for his commissions. Many of his collectors took advantage of these "bargains," and the published results of the auction undoubtedly influenced subsequent sales of Hill's large canvases.[84]

NEW SUBJECTS

Following his auction, Hill took a summer trip to Utah, where he spent at least a month before returning to San Francisco by early August.[85] In transit, Hill may have recorded the charming *Near Lake Tahoe* (fig. 38), another example of his continuing fondness for High Sierra views. He did not draw upon his sketches from this trip for paintings he exhibited in the fall, which included White Mountain subjects and a scene of Cascade Lake.

These, with Hill's other entries in the state fair art exhibition, were met with conflicting responses in local art columns. The *Call* stated that "his pictures bear the stamp of genius in the most enviable qualities of a true artist—beauty, grandeur, and originality." At about the same time, the *Daily Evening Post* cited Hill's work as "artistically handled," but lacking poetry. The *Post* reviewer, however, praised "the 'Eagle Picture,' as it is called," but called the artist's Yosemite scenes for Ralston "failures. They are weak, starchy, and somewhat coarsely treated. The artist seems to have been aware that his patron was a better judge of bank checks than of oil paintings, and has conducted himself accordingly."[86]

Although the quality of the sketches undertaken for Ralston belies the reviewer's appraisal, the length of time Hill took to complete this commission suggests these large paintings were not executed with his usual ease. Whatever the circumstances, the results were not as well-received as the critically praised and innovative *Home of the Eagle*.

Hill's decision to give *Home of the Eagle* and other new subjects (such as *Cascade Lake*) greater prominence in exhibitions may reflect a concerted effort to develop audiences for new views. His attempts to broaden his subjects and creatively market his work, even using strategies that involved financial and critical risks, indicate that he was unable to rely on gallery sales and commissions for a secure income from his art work, even in 1874, when he was arguably San Francisco's best-known painter and the local art market was still relatively robust.

Hill's September pronouncement of his intention to create a large painting of the driving of the last spike of the Transcontinental Railroad confirms his eagerness to explore new subjects and offers an explanation for his summer travels in Utah. The canvas, celebrating a recent accomplishment that could be associated with national interests and technological progress, would have appealed to a number of San Francisco business leaders, and held the promise of the immense popularity that greeted the *Great Cañon of the Sierra, Yosemite* when it was exhibited three years earlier.

The subject may have attracted Hill as a departure from his recent endeavors and as a creative challenge. Whether he was capable of depicting this monumental historic event was publicly debated: "Such a picture will require a versatility of talent which but few possess. The only large figure piece we now remember to have seen by him was 'Shylock,'" —a reference to *The Merchant of Venice* scene Hill had exhibited nearly a decade earlier.[87]

In early fall 1874, the ambitious *The Driving of the Last Spike* project was delayed when Hill became ill, and traveled to San Mateo County, south of San Francisco, to recover under a physician's care. Though he had received support from the press his auction in the spring, Hill now was presented as an artist easily distracted from painting by other interests, despite periods of intense productivity. While away, he reportedly spent considerable time hunting quail (one of his favorite repasts), causing one critic to hope that "he has found time to put aside the gun long enough to collect objects for some of those wood and mountain scenes he so well knows how to reproduce on canvas." Hill may have been further diverted from his studio when he became a partner in the art gallery of Joseph Roos in November, another step taken, quite likely, to further supplement his income.[88]

His convalescence in the rural San Francisco Peninsula may have resulted in one of Hill's more unusual compositions, *Irrigating at Strawberry Farm* (fig. 39). Although generally considered to have been produced in the 1860s, this engaging study—like most of Hill's oil sketches—is undated. The tonality of the painting, treatment of trees in the middle distance, and adept depiction of the foreground blossoms with "dots" of paint, suggest it was executed following Hill's return to California. Masterfully organized in a series of horizontal and diagonal planes, *Irrigating at Strawberry Farm* is remarkable for its agricultural subject and multiple figures, including both Asian and non-Asian laborers in the presence of a well-groomed landowner or foreman. Because Hill rarely produced works of this type, the treatment may have been suggested by a patron or the piece conceived as a gift to acknowledge hospitality. No evidence of a larger painting of the subject exists, confounding efforts to determine its date and history with greater certainty.

Continuing his predilection for new subject matter, Hill entered two oval-topped Swiss landscapes in the January 1875 Art Association exhibition. These paintings and a scene of the Forest of Fontainebleau displayed the previous year, are among his earliest documented European views.

Hill's major painting of the winter was an eight-by-twelve-foot view of the Sierra Nevada mountains that was either commissioned or purchased by E. J. "Lucky" Baldwin. Once more, Hill received a substantial sum (reportedly

$10,000) for a huge canvas from a wealthy businessman. *In the Heart of the Sierra* evoked Frederic Church not only in its title (one of his best-known works was called *The Heart of the Andes*), but in its depiction of a generalized subject composed from a number of oil sketches.[89] The use of this procedure, associated with the immensely popular Church and Bierstadt, was uncommon for Hill.

The painting's exhibition in San Francisco also represented a departure, as, in a break from tradition, it was installed at the Art Association while the School of Design was in session. Even though *In the Heart of the Sierra* was recognized as a highly-accomplished work by an artist of stature, the special treatment Hill received from the Art Association was duly (and critically) noted in the local press.[90]

In the following months, a number of other skeptical comments arose about Hill's activities. Although criticisms of his paintings had appeared alongside accolades in newspaper art commentaries for some time, they now took on a more personal tone. Hill may well have been involved in struggles within the Board of the Art Association (he was not re-elected vice president), and a report that he was considering a return East (due to poor health) questioned whether the commissions Hill said he held there actually existed.[91]

AN EASTERN TRIP

The Eastern trip Hill planned for early 1875 was scaled back from an extended stay ("of about a year's duration"), delayed throughout the spring, and finally realized as a "brief visit" to Boston in June. Its purposes were to sketch White Mountain scenes and to acquire Eastern paintings for resale at Joseph Roos and Co.—logical goals given Hill's financial situation and San Francisco's then lackluster art market.[92] Hill had exhibited his oil sketches in California in May, probably in an effort to offer reasonably priced work for sale. And because Leland Stanford had recently declined to commit to the purchase of the *The Driving of the Last Spike,* it would have been particularly important for Hill to seek other income at the time.[93]

His visit to Massachusetts therefore offered Hill both fresh material and the opportunity to stimulate the marketplace by introducing art work from the East to San Francisco clients. Another reason for Hill's journey was conjectured by the *News Letter* in a somewhat mean-spirited notice that closed:

> Mr. Hill leaves for the East in a few days to ramble among the White Mountains, where he hopes to find rest and quiet from business cares for a few weeks. It is hoped that he will, while there, feel equal to the task of painting some of those charming Eastern wood scenes from Nature. It must be a strain upon an artist to produce so many pictures from memory, but then we have known artists who essayed large Yosemite views from points which they had never visited, but which their friend, the photographer, had. This may be considered a still greater strain—of the imagination.[94]

His several weeks in the East, with both a change of scenery and a well-received showing of his paintings at Williams & Everett galleries, offered Hill a respite. The *Boston Evening Transcript* characterized his landscapes as having "almost extraordinary" textures, and compared one to the paintings of Narcisse Diaz.[95]

Hill undoubtedly joined friends in the East on sketching trips into the nearby countryside. It is likely that *Flashpoint* (fig. 40), which is dated 1875, was a product of this visit. Although its landscape eludes precise identification, the foliage appears to be typical of New England. Hill was fond of hunting, and the hunter shown with his dogs may represent the artist himself. As with his best oil sketches of this period, the foreground is developed with relatively loose brushstrokes, and small touches of paint bring details to attention.

Other oil sketches probably made in the East include *Forest Interior* (fig. 41) and *Artist at his Easel in the Woods* (see page 10). The former beautifully renders the effects of the diffuse mid-day sun, lighting conditions that Hill preferred to those of the more dramatic early morning and sunset.

Artist at his Easel in the Woods, likely painted as a token of friendship, offers significant information on the conduct of oil sketching trips during the 1870s. The dark complected and mustachioed central figure seated painting among birch trees is probably a sketching companion. The collapsible easel is set up and a painting—perhaps on canvas—is well underway. Set-ups such as this—or in lieu of easels, boxes that accommodated standard-sized

sketching paper—allowed artists to easily and directly record woodland scenes like this one. Hill's treatment of the woods in this sketch and in *Forest Interior* is quite similar to that in the oil sketches made by Worthington Whittredge in the Catskills at this time. They, too, have been adjudged as "intended to be complete, self-standing works in themselves." [96]

BUSINESS AND ART IN SAN FRANCISCO

Hill was in high spirits upon his return to San Francisco at the end of July, "resuming his studies in geology—sketching Bulls and Bears on California street." This is undoubtedly a reference to the investment activities Hill undertook with vigor and mixed success in subsequent years. [97] He also participated in auctions and exhibited small paintings of White Mountain scenery at Snow and Roos in the late fall.

Among the works he auctioned at this time was a small painting titled *Moonlight Trout Fishing*, probably related to the small oil on canvas titled *Night Fishing, Lake Tahoe* (fig. 42). The scene, in which two fishermen attract trout to the surface while their companions guide the boat under a rising full moon, is similar to one, with elements reversed, painted by Bierstadt. Hill's sketch, likely inspired by Bierstadt's work, may have served as a study for the larger canvas offered by Hill in his 1882 auction sale.[98]

By November 1875, Hill had completed his six-by-ten-foot painting *Donner Lake,* commissioned by Leland Stanford to embellish his mansion under construction on Nob Hill. The project, for which Hill had made sketches many months before, is proof that patronage in San Francisco had not ceased, and that Hill's work continued to be appreciated. Local reviews favorably compared Hill's interpretation with Bierstadt's, surely augmenting the respect in which he was held.[99]

At the beginning of 1876, Hill was preparing for the Centennial Exhibition in Philadelphia, for which he had completed another mammoth-sized painting of Yosemite (fig. 43). His new composition and *Donner Lake* (which he would send East, along with *Home of the Eagle*) drew attention in the Art Association's Winter Exhibition. They were credited as "in Mr. Hill's best style, and we have long regarded him as one of the first landscape painters of the age."[100]

At the same time, Hill was criticized for painting his third scene of Yosemite from the same viewpoint, and for nearly replicating a previous work (*Great Cañon of the Sierra, Yosemite*) that had been sold for a substantial sum.[101] Actually, *Yosemite Valley* differed significantly from the earlier painting in both palette and viewpoint.

The next week the *News Letter* lauded *Donner Lake,* but followed that appreciation with an anonymous entry echoing the veiled accusation published the previous summer. The writer asserted that prior to executing the painting, Hill had not visited the site of the view presented in *Great Cañon of the Sierra, Yosemite,* and contended that it had been composed after a photograph by Watkins (figs. 19, 20). The note continued that *Yosemite Valley* differed significantly from its predecessor in that Hill had visited and sketched the scene in the interim.[102]

Two other paintings that Hill entered in the exhibition, referred to as "Nature and Art," also earned notice. "Mr. Hill has far more versatility of talent than he often gets credit for, and we know he has much which is never drawn upon. . . . Like most artists, he paints that which is creditable and which pays best.[103]

At the time, art sales were languishing in San Francisco, with one journal describing the near impossibility of dealing "foreign work," and relating Hill's unsuccessful efforts to sell paintings acquired in the East the previous summer.[104] This experience did not discourage Hill, for in May 1876 he bought Joseph Roos's gallery, becoming its sole proprietor. Renamed Thomas Hill & Co., the establishment continued to sell prints (including chromolithographs) and art supplies, as well as work by both "local and foreign artists."[105]

It is likely that Hill involved one or more of his sons in the management of his business. His growing family included nine children, several of whom were reaching adulthood. Their assistance would have been required to operate the store, as Hill was often away from San Francisco. That year, for instance, he left on a sketching trip "in the country" in late July, and departed for Philadelphia in September.[106]

At the California State Fair in August, both Hill and his contemporary Edwin Deakin exhibited Wasatch Mountain scenes described as being "as different as can be," with the reviewer observing that "one or both must have painted it from imagination, and it would be pertinent just here to ask when did either Mr. Hill or Mr. Deakin visit the Wasatch Mountains?"[107] As the subjects of the small paintings Hill had been exhibiting were not locations he had visited during the preceding years, it seems likely he was now producing sketches, as well as larger canvases, in his studio.

Hill probably indulged in this practice for many years afterward as well, though it is very difficult to distinguish his small paintings produced on the spot from those produced elsewhere. Revealingly, at least one oil sketch is marked with a location that is distant from its subject, and Hill's records show he made and sold multiple copies of certain views long after he had visited them.[108]

FIGURE 43
Thomas Hill
Yosemite Valley, 1876.
Oil on canvas, 72 x 120 in.
Oakland Museum of California; gift of the Kahn Foundation.

THE CENTENNIAL EXHIBITION

Although the Centennial Exhibition was well underway when Hill left for the East in mid-September, 1876, he was away nearly two months. The sight of his exhibition-size paintings hanging alongside those of Bierstadt, Thomas Moran, and other leading artists of the day must have been gratifying. In addition, the gold medal, the highest award for landscape painting, bestowed on Hill for his *Donner Lake, Home of the Eagle,* and *Yosemite Valley* was a rare tangible recognition of national esteem.

Hill's success may have inspired him, upon his return to California in November, to predict that he would quickly finish nine paintings. His failure to participate in a sale of paintings by local artists at Newhall's gallery in December, however, suggests that his prophecy was not realized. The *News Letter* wondered about the absence of his work, asking, "What if Mr. Hill *is* flushed with his victory won at Philadelphia, is he not a resident artist? Has he no ideas above self-interest?"[109]

Certainly the imprimatur of his Centennial Exposition award reinforced Hill's position of leadership among California artists, even as a number of capable painters were now working in San Francisco. B. E. Lloyd, in *Lights and Shades in San Francisco,* listed Keith, Williams, Norton Bush, William Hahn, and William Marple among the city's leading talents, but identified Hill as "foremost," saying

> His paintings are noted for their richness and brilliancy of color, and their bold and broad style of execution—having the reality and solidity of nature, that is so difficult to express on a flat piece of canvas. . . . The Yosemite Valley is his favorite haunt—his largest and finest pictures being of that locality.[110]

Though glowing, this assessment ignored the many other landscape subjects undertaken and the different formats used by Hill. The close association of the artist with monumental Yosemite views may have been beneficial, but must have hampered Hill's efforts to explore and market new subjects at the same time.

This predicament continued to challenge Hill in 1877. Although he completed a large painting of Purissima Falls (in San Mateo County south of San Francisco) in January, its theme was viewed as unequal to his abilities:

> It is to be regretted that Mr. Hill's first pictures, after his victory at Philadelphia, should have been first a still life, and now a subject necessarily forbidding the exercise of his highest talents. They, however, tend to show that this artist can make a good showing with any subject.[111]

A SECOND AUCTION

Despite the mixed critical response his paintings received on the heels of his success in Philadelphia, the auction Hill staged at galleries of the Art Association three months later indicated he was struggling to sell his paintings. The *News Letter* noted this situation and defended Hill's use of the school for this purpose, arguing that he had long exhibited with the Art Association, despite realizing few sales there.[112]

Within an apathetic art market, Hill presented ninety paintings for sale in April, 1877. The preview exhibition was well-attended and, as with Hill's previous sales, the event drew extensive newspaper coverage. Again, the public was admonished that "this will be the last of his pictures to be sold here for years; he intends to paint hereafter for sale elsewhere, his work being in demand in the East."[113]

The auction itself, which included paintings of a variety of sizes and subjects, was disappointing. Accounts vary, but the bidding was characterized as "so-so at best" and sales apparently totaled only $7,500. One report, in fact, claimed that the sale was stopped, with prices failing to meet even the costs of the artist's materials. The event clearly did not fulfill Hill's expectations. Sales held by fellow artists Marple and Gideon Jacques Denny in the following weeks were likewise unsuccessful, and led one newspaper to judge that "a picture sale at the present time is really and only a slaughterhouse of art."[114]

FIGURE 44
Thomas Hill
Source of Paper Mill Creek, Woodacre,
ca. 1874.
Oil on paper mounted on board, 14 x 21 in.
Private collection.

Shortly thereafter, Virgil Williams resigned as director of the School of Design, and Hill withdrew as a member of the Art Association's Committee on the School of Design in response. The dispute was apparently quickly resolved, and Williams rescinded his action. Although Hill did not attend the committee's mid-May meeting (he had been absent often), he reportedly had re-assumed his position with the group.[115] Perhaps seeking solace from the tensions of the preceding weeks, Hill was reported at St. Helena in early June, most likely with Williams, "for a few weeks diversion and study." From there, he traveled north to Mendocino County to make sketches.[116]

This trip was brief, as by mid-June Hill announced his intentions to travel East and to sell his art store. Speculation abounded that the paintings he had failed to sell in San Francisco would be sent to New York "with a view to their sale to Eastern connoisseurs." The reporter observed that "art interests of every character are very dull here just now, hence the exodus of so many artists and the retirement of so many dealers."[117] Certainly, the state of San Francisco's art market was quite fragile prior to the end of the 1870s, an additional challenge to artists working in California.

MOUNT SHASTA PAINTINGS

Although Hill's activities portended a lengthy stay away, there is no evidence of an Eastern trip that summer. Instead, following the exhibition of his highly-praised painting of Lake Ralphine at the end of June, Hill left on a sketching trip to Mount Shasta. He was back by late July "with plenty of material for

fresh pictures." In commenting on the new studies, one source wrote that "Mr. Hill always sketches in colors—a rare thing for American artists and not marvelously common in any country. Beneath the cloudless skies and during the long unvarying days of California it can be done with greater convenience than elsewhere. . . . Hill not only has the steadiness of our atmospheric effects to assist him, but that quickness of execution that enables him to finish a sketch at a sitting and be sure that his work is an absolute reproduction of nature."[118]

Hill's fondness for Mount Shasta and its environs is manifest in a number of lovely oil sketches made on different occasions. A prominent feature in Northern California, and important spiritually to Native Americans nearby, Mount Shasta engaged Hill's interest for some time. His interpretations of this area range from simplified views of the mountain peak against an intense blue sky, to scenes such as *Black Butte, Mount Shasta* and *Mount Shasta from Castle Lake* (figs. 45, 46) that emphasize the foreground as much as the imposing mountain. The area also afforded excellent trout fishing, a pastime he continued to represent in appealing small format works (fig. 47).

Black Butte, Mount Shasta is an unusual composition for Hill in its use of receding vertical elements to lead the viewer into the picture. Lively rabbits at the lower left contrast with the foreground stump and the dead pine tree at center. *Mount Shasta from Castle Lake* shows a very different view in which a rugged hillside frames the mountain. Its immensity contrasts markedly with Hill's more intimate *Black Butte* and Sisson's scenes (see following pages). The scene was probably created as a study for a larger canvas, or may have been executed later in preparation for *Picturesque California.*

Hill's oil sketch of *Sisson's Inn, near Mount Shasta* (fig. 48), a well known lodging in the area, offers considerable detail in the buildings and trees, and features deftly and broadly painted foreground areas. It, too, may date from the 1877 visit. The work is striking in its freshness, and provides an example (at

the lower right) of Hill's technique of "scraping off instead of layering on color" to describe textures.[119] *Farm at Mount Shasta (Sisson's Inn)* (fig. 49) also depicts a group of structures, this time clustered beneath the imposing peak. This composition (possibly a gift to the owner of the establishment) differs from *Sisson's Inn, near Mount Shasta* in its summary rendition and its color scheme.

The importance of Mount Shasta to Hill is suggested by his immediate use of his oil sketches from his July 1877 trip. Shortly after his return, he was

FIGURE 46
Thomas Hill
Mount Shasta from Castle Lake, ca. 1888.
Oil on board, 14 x 21 in.
The Gilcrease Museum, Tulsa, Oklahoma.

FIGURE 47
Thomas Hill
Trout Fishing, 1877.
Oil on paper mounted on board, 14 x 18 in.
Private collection.

commissioned to replace paintings that had been destroyed by a fire at the Lick House, a local hostelry of some note.[120] Hill's contributions included *Mount Shasta from Sisson's.*

Although the oil studies from the trip were impressive, the paintings of Mount Shasta and the two Yosemite scenes for the Lick House were criticized as too hastily painted when exhibited at the Art Association in mid-September. Each measured six by ten feet and all were finished in under six weeks, for an agreed price of $500 apiece.[121] Despite Hill's acknowledged skills as a rapid sketcher, he hardly could have been expected to give these enormous compositions detailed attention in such little time, and the sum offered provided little incentive for protracted labor.

FINANCIAL UNCERTAINTIES

Hill again was foundering in his efforts to commercially promote his work. In September 1877 he was one of the few San Francisco artists to participate in the Mechanics' Fair exhibition, others abstaining to protest the large number of foreign paintings being included. After initially supporting the boycott, Hill entered a number of the paintings from his spring auction at the last moment, hoping to collect a $250 award designated for a local artist.[122] Hill also exhibited a large painting of Mount Shasta, begun some months before, to generally good reviews.[123]

Hill's second exhibition-size painting of Mount Shasta continued his efforts to present new California subjects to the public. The challenges of finding a market, however, were summed up at the year's end:

> Christmas in the year of our lord 1877 dawns upon the dullest art season Californians have ever witnessed. Local art is gone out of sight utterly; we hear no more of sales at good prices by Keith, Hill, Brookes and others of our local celebrities, and as regards foreign pictures, there has been, for the last half of the year, absolutely nothing to note worth speaking of.[124]

This assessment is followed by news that Hill had begun painting *The Driving of the Last Spike,* with a note that "Mr. Hill has heretofore been known as a landscape painter, and if he now succeeds in a different line, he will win fresh and most desirable laurels."[125] Hill undoubtedly saw the *The Driving of the Last Spike* as a vehicle to improve his skills in another branch of painting and to expand the subject matter with which he was identified.

Hill sent his son Edward to Portland, Oregon, in January 1878 in a hapless effort to sell work. The *News Letter* reported that

> The Portlanders failed to appreciate the offering, just as our art collectors did, for it was the same lot put up at auction in the Art Association Gallery last season. . . . According to the Portland papers, but *four* pictures were sold, and they brought infinitesimal prices, in comparison to the value placed on them by the artist.[126]

These fruitless efforts and his desperation to place work were damaging to Hill:

FIGURE 48
Thomas Hill
Sisson's Inn, near Mount Shasta, n.d.
Oil on paper, 14 x 21 in.
Private collection.

FIGURE 49
Thomas Hill
Farm at Mount Shasta (Sisson's Inn), n.d.
Oil on paper, 13 x 20 in.
Candace McKee Ashmun.

> Does it not seem strange that an artist, who has made sales of a goodly number of paintings to our citizens at excellent prices, should thus hawk his works over the country, and sell them for what they will bring on the auction block. No wonder buyers are shy of local art when a painting—for which six hundred dollars is demanded, and for similar works, time and again, from five to six hundred dollars has been received—is sold in a neighboring city for one hundred and thirty dollars, including a frame, which must have cost not less than fifty dollars.[127]

Clearly, even near the height of his reputation, Hill could not achieve financial success by the sale of his art work in the economic environment of the late 1870s.

Hill's paintings of early 1878, *Castle Rocks* and *Headwaters of the McCloud River,* were scenes from the Mount Shasta area. Both were well-liked by the press, and one critic suggested San Francisco's depressed economy had inspired Hill and other artists to work harder and thus achieve greater accomplishments. Hill was credited with greater harmony and delicacy of tones in his new paintings. Whatever the reason, the McCloud River composition sold quickly.[128]

In the spring of 1878, Hill's energy was consumed by his continued work on the monumental *The Driving of the Last Spike.* Though several oil sketches relating to the project are listed in the sales catalogues for Hill's estate, few if any still exist. Further, it is more likely that he relied on photographs for the many portraits demanded by this unusual composition. The project, on which Hill worked erratically for the next several years, appears to have taken precedence over his sketching trip that season.

Hill again was rumored to be contemplating an extended trip East, but instead left San Francisco in early July 1878 to paint around Mount Hood and Mount Rainier. He was away nearly six weeks, reportedly returning with many sketches of rocks and trees from Oregon and studies of the Puyallup Valley in Washington Territory. Perhaps the fine view of *Mount Hood* in the collection of the Pittock Mansion (fig. 50) resulted from this trip; it demonstrates the subtleties of color and treatment with which Hill was then being credited, and reflects Hill's expressed interest at the time in brighter compositions.[129] A challenging subject due to its relatively precipitous rise from the surrounding landscape, the peak is effectively anchored by Hill using foothills and the foliage on either side of the river cutting through the foreground. The relationship of the sketch to a larger painting by Hill suggests that it served as a study for him (fig. 51).

SUCCESS IN THE STOCK MARKET

In October, the *News Letter* called upon Hill and William Keith, who was also becoming a prominent resident artist, to develop their oil sketches from the summer for exhibition. There was a suggestion, however, that Hill's art had been subordinated to his new found interest (and apparent success) in the stock market, noting that Hill:

[is] quite absorbed in the pursuit of wealth in this direction, and that all his beautiful sketches, taken during his recent trip North, are not being utilized at present. The same authority gives his winnings at from ten to eighty thousand dollars.[130]

Although Hill surely was not alone among San Francisco painters in making investments (and may have influenced others to pursue this source of income), he seems to have realized more substantial profits. His biographical sketch in the 1878 *Pacific Coast Mining Review* made reference to the allure of the market:

> The transcript of mountains, woods and lakes, however, sometimes for a period becomes with our subject a matter of less inspiration than the changes and excitements of the Stock Exchange. The profits of a few hundred shares of Sierra Nevada . . . has the tendency to quench for a time the light of the pencil.[131]

Even if they consumed his energy, Hill's stock transactions were also remunerative, and may have allowed him to spend more time working in the studio than at generating sales.[132]

This upswing in his financial fortunes helped Hill to move into a new studio in the Nevada Block in early 1879. He also sold his art gallery to Snow and Company, and his wife purchased "a twenty room house on a ten acre estate of Seminary Avenue in Oakland."[133]

INFLUENCE ON OTHER ARTISTS

In early 1879, Hill worked on landscapes of Mount Hood and Howard's cattle ranch in San Mateo from oil sketches, and a portrait of two of his daughters. He exhibited all to acclaim, and was again declared "the leading artist of the Pacific coast." Hill's powers as a painter at this time are demonstrated in the glorious canvas *California* that he had on display that spring.[134]

Hill is not known to have taken on many students, despite his stature, close friendship with Virgil Williams at the School of Design, and times of apparent financial need. The high regard in which his work was held certainly brought attention to his paintings in San Francisco. But despite press comments to the effect that "Tom Hill's style is too generally imitated," and that his school "represents in good, bad and indifferent ways San Francisco art," his impact on the styles of other major artists of the day appears to have been minimal.[135]

The styles of younger artists, such as Keith and Arthur F. Mathews, evinced very different temperaments, and even the paintings of Williams, who often accompanied Hill sketching, are quite distinctive. Exceptions tend to be artists who are relatively unknown today, such as Nellie Hopps, who exhibited paintings in her studio in 1879. Many of these were made on sketching trips Hopps took while a student at the School of Design, and they were characterized as "a little in Hill's manner, but all of them show individuality and talent of a high order."[136]

A comparison of their respective treatments of *Paper Mill Creek* in Marin County, however, suggests that Hill's influence on Hopps was substan-

FIGURE 52
Thomas Hill
Paper Mill Creek, n.d.
Oil on paper mounted on panel,
14 x 20½ in.
Fine Arts Museums of San Francisco;
Mildred Anna Williams Collection.

FIGURE 53
Nellie Hopps (United States, 1855–1956)
Taylor Paper Mill, Taylorsville, Marin County,
n.d.
Oil on canvas mounted on masonite,
18 x 30 in.
California Historical Society, San Francisco.

tial (figs. 52, 53). Their scenes are nearly identical, and it may be surmised that they were painted at the same time, most likely between 1877 and 1879, with Hopps closely following Hill's example. Despite Hopps' efforts to imitate his work, Hill clearly created the more dynamic composition. One of his most inspired oil sketches, the crisply-rendered view shows the first paper mill in the West.[137] In depicting the historic structure, Hill effectively created a center of light by embedding the white mill in foliage, with the river reinforcing it as a center of focus. By this time a practiced landscape artist, Hill also utilized a number of devices that he had recommended to his son, including "never bring a tree into the foreground of a picture unless you carry it out of the picture at the top."[138]

YOSEMITE REVISITED

Hill left San Francisco in the spring of 1879 on his annual sketching tour, this time traveling to Yosemite. This was his first venture there in several years, and reportedly was undertaken in response to requests by patrons for more

Yosemite scenery. His departure prompted an accusation that he had "depend[ed] more upon photographs than original sketches for his Yosemite pictures," and the hope that "after six months respite from the labors of the studio, he has again put on the armor and gone forth to interpret nature on canvas with some of the strength he possessed before neglecting his chosen and well-suited profession—art.[139]

Hill's trip revived his interest in Yosemite. He stayed longer than anticipated, and put his new sketches to use immediately upon his return. The sojourn yielded some thirty to forty works on paper,

> proof that his time has not been misspent. These were all taken in oil on the spot, and will be new even to those most familiar with the gallery by personal observation, or by photographic illustrations. He has done his best to wander out of the beaten track of the tourist or the artist with the camera. To look through his sketches is like a visit to the wonderful valley.[140]

Within two weeks of arriving back in San Francisco, Hill had completed and sold a painting of Diamond Cascade, in the Little Yosemite Valley, and was embarked on other Yosemite scenes. Reflecting a change, only one of these larger compositions—destined for the parlor of the Palace Hotel, where General Grant was staying—offered an overview of Yosemite Valley from Inspiration Point. Hill was developing new approaches to the valley, and vowed to "represent it only in fragments—the only way, he says, in which its successful representation is possible."[141]

Oil sketches such as *Indian Camp, Yosemite Valley* (fig. 54) or *Sentinel Rock, Yosemite* (fig. 55) may date from about this time. Both are rendered in high-toned, bright colors and isolate specific Yosemite "fragments," and in each a path or stones in the foreground offer viewers access into the composition. The intimate scale of *Indian Camp, Yosemite Valley* is effective, and the immediacy of its execution is shown in the small daubs of color used to signify faces as well as landscape elements.[142] The foreground of *Sentinel Rock, Yosemite* is also freely treated, with bravura brushwork that appears almost abstract. Sentinel Rock is projected against the clear blue midday sky, endowing the monolith with a commanding presence, despite the small format of the work.

Yosemite views occupied Hill through much of the fall of 1879, and his industriousness was noted in the face of a slow market that discouraged many artists.[143] By early November, however, his interest in this subject had waned, and Hill reportedly

hid away all the results of his summer tour to Yosemite, and has turned again with what there is left in him of taste and intellectual vigor to elaborating the sketches of his Oregon tour, and to remodeling one or two wood interiors.[144]

DEPARTURE FROM SAN FRANCISCO

Shortly thereafter, Hill moved his studio from his Nevada Block quarters to his home in Oakland. Although his new house was spacious, it seems that the relocation was motivated by financial reasons, as he was now encumbered with a large mortgage. A gregarious individual, who from all accounts enjoyed playing host to artists, critics, and patrons in his studios, Hill had countenanced distractions to his work for years. By moving across the Bay to paint, he became isolated from many San Francisco colleagues and activities.

Hill's remove and the continued doldrums in the local art market were reported in the *Chronicle* at year's end:

> In the studios of other artists, there is not much doing, only the quiet plodding that is rather a result of habit than of the expectation of reward. Hill is presumed to be hard at work at home in Oakland, though his distance precludes accurate information.[145]

Art sales in California came to a virtual standstill in 1880, but Hill continued to produce outstanding paintings of new subjects. In March, his *The Salmon Festival,* which was prominently displayed in the Art Association's spring exhibition, drew critical notice. Its unusual subject, probably recorded in sketches Hill made on his trip north in 1878 (fig. 56), was described as

> a curious custom of the Vancouver Indians. At the beginning of the salmon season the first fish taken is brought to the encampment and presented to the medicine man, who eats it, the occasion being one of general rejoicing among the tribe.[146]

FIGURE 56
Thomas Hill
The Salmon Festival, Columbia River,
ca. 1888.
Oil on paper mounted on canvas, 11 x 15 in.
Foundation for the Preservation of the
Governor's Mansion, Olympia, Washington.

Despite its engaging theme, *The Salmon Festival* was also criticized for the apparent haste with which it was painted and its "monotonous color."[147]

Although remarkably similar in its delineation of the canoes and surrounding cliffs, Hill's oil sketch of the same subject exhibits vibrant color and a more effective composition. It shows fewer figures (and omits elements such as a small dog in the left foreground), while the more compactly placed canoes and bright glaciers that define the mountains in the background enliven the scene. If, in fact, this was the study Hill used for his larger painting (which it certainly appears to be), the comparison illustrates Hill's talent in making sketches outdoors, and underscores the challenges entailed in translating small scale images to larger formats.

The dormant art market undoubtedly exacerbated Hill's feelings of uncertainty about the direction his painting should take at this time. The *News Letter* advised that

> It is evident that for some time past Mr. Hill's mantle as an eminent landscape painter has not set easily upon him. He seems, from his later exhibits, to be going back to his original intent, that of a figure painter.[148]

This is in apparent reference not only to *The Salmon Festival* and the portraits of his daughters that Hill had on view, but also to the fact that he was believed to be completing the *The Driving of the Last Spike* in his Oakland studio.

In May 1880, with rumors circulating that he had not sold a painting in eight months, Hill reportedly planned a trip to England. Instead, he travelled to Boston in mid-June, then made an extended sketching tour in the White Mountains, whose inspiration is recorded in scenes such as *Cathedral Ledge, North Conway, New Hampshire* (fig. 57).

Hill remained in the East until early October, when he wrote of plans to move his family to New York and reside there "for two years at least."[149] Such a departure would have coincided with a general exodus of artists from San Francisco that had begun. For some reason—perhaps his wife and children objected or he further assessed his career options—Hill did not act on this proposal. His predicted "brief" return to California at the end of "an unprecedentally bad 'off' year" for artists, was instead permanent except for his customary summer sketching trips and travel required by commissions.[150]

THE DRIVING OF THE LAST SPIKE

In late January 1881, *The Driving of the Last Spike* (fig. 58), after many delays, was put on exhibition at the Art Association gallery. The elaborate scene, with over three hundred figures (sixty of them portraits), represented an immensely difficult subject to convey effectively on canvas. Although the groupings and three-dimensionality of the figures drew high praise, critics countered that

> when people came, at last, to behold a group of gentlemen, standing with that stiff awkwardness . . . upon a railroad track in the middle of the desert, there was an inevitable sense of disappointment.[151]

That Hill had allowed the painting to languish due to the challenges it posed and because there was no patron at hand was reiterated in the press.[152] By the time he finally completed and presented the work in 1881, large "history" paintings were generally out of fashion, particularly in the East where Winslow Homer and Thomas Eakins were rising to prominence as figure painters. Further, the mammoth size of *The Driving of the Last Spike* limited potential purchasers. Its display in San Francisco and Sacramento yielded no buyers, and the *The Driving of the Last Spike* was returned to Hill's studio to remain (along with *The Salmon Festival,* other large paintings, and many oil sketches) in the artist's possession until the time of his death.[153]

With his energy directed at the completion and exhibition of *The Driving of the Last Spike,* Hill displayed few additional pieces in San Francisco in early 1881. The only other large painting from his easel was a scene of birches, probably from studies made in the East. The reviewer for *Wasp* commented

FIGURE 58
Thomas Hill
The Driving of the Last Spike, 1881.
Oil on canvas, 96 x 144½ in.
California State Railroad Museum,
Sacramento.

favorably on its appearance in the Art Association's spring exhibition, and added that

> The display of sketches by Clenewerck, Hill, Rix, Straus, Deakin, Tavernier, Yelland, and others, is the most interesting feature of the exhibition. The pictures attract a brief inspection, but the sketches can be studied for hours. There is apparent in them the out-of-doors nature that somehow fails to get into many pictures by the same artists, and this is notably true of Clenewerck and Straus, and in a less degree of Hill, Rix and the rest.[154]

This statement of critical appreciation for his oil sketches would have been small solace for Hill given the cool reception for his *The Driving of the Last Spike*. His efforts to revive his fortunes through figure painting had miscarried, and Hill at the age of fifty-two was likely less resilient than in earlier years. At the outset of the summer of 1881, he retreated to Yosemite "to busy himself in his studio at Mariposa, practically retiring from a field he could command if he chose."[155] In Yosemite, he could maintain an independent studio less expensively while having access to tourists ready to purchase mementos of their Sierra travels.

By late July, however, Hill was again in the East, occupying rooms at the Profile House, a famous White Mountain hotel, for nearly a month. He and fellow guest H. A. Ferguson, a distinguished New York landscape painter, joined Hill's brother Edward in sketching the area around Franconia Notch.[156]

A Disappointing Sale

Although Hill exhibited scenes of Yosemite, the White Mountains, and Washington Territory upon his return to California that fall, he otherwise earned little mention in the press until March 1882. That month, he offered up 129 paintings, half of which were oil sketches, for another auction. The sale was promoted as featuring paintings that had not been on the market previously, although several of the major pieces, among them the large *Mount Shasta* and *The Salmon Festival*, had been on prior public display.

A measure of the artist's outlook was his decision to offer many works, larger paintings as well as sketches, unframed. Hill's explanation was that "a great part of the paintings now purchased in this city are for Eastern account" and that art collectors often chose to frame their acquisitions in "various and fantastic" styles. His acknowledgement that "a painting is improved by a rich frame," however, suggests that the more likely factors were the cost of frames and Hill's lack of optimism for the forthcoming event.[157]

Press notices for the auction emphasized the large number of sketches that were available, even though these had comprised an even greater percentage of works offered at his earlier auctions. The oils on paper were highly praised:

> Artists generally decline selling their sketches, on the ground—first that they are their stock in trade, so to say, from which to produce large pictures, and next, that purchasers are apt to say: "Oh, that's only a sketch," and pass on; but Mr. Hill's sketches are more, much more than this; they

are finished pictures. The rapidity with which he manipulates color enables him to complete a sketch while an ordinary artist is surveying the scene and drawing outlines. This enables him to seize the opportunity offered by brilliant and short-lived effects, and to take advantage of all the opportunities offered to him by his master—Nature.[158]

Significantly, buyers were no longer cautioned that Hill was encumbered with commissions and that future opportunities to acquire his work would be rare.

Hill's first large public sale in five years earned favorable newspaper accounts, and attendance was reportedly high despite foul weather. The audience was described as appreciative, and the offerings included an extraordinary variety of views. *Profile Lake, Franconia Notch, New Hampshire*; *Paper Mill Creek*; and *The Olympic Range, Victoria, British Columbia* were among many scenes of the White Mountains, Mount Shasta, Yosemite, and the Northwest in the sketches proffered, and the oil paintings included such views as the *Garden of the Gods in Colorado* and *The Conservatory Window*.

Unfortunately, sales results were mixed at best. While all of the sketches reportedly sold, bidding failed to reach the reserve set on several of the larger paintings (including *Mount Shasta*), and Hill was characterized as disappointed with the results.

The paintings presented richly represented Hill's work, even if they were roundly criticized by some reviewers. In placing such a collection before the public, Hill made himself vulnerable, a fact noted in a *San Francisco Examiner* article:

> Not even so favored and talented an artist as Mr. Hill can afford to give his works so promiscuously, with the good and the bad mixed, to the public. . . . That he cheapens his work as well as himself, by exposing for sale paintings that bring half of what others have paid in regular sale, is self-evident. An artist ought to be progressive, and if Mr. Hill received $5,000 for a picture the size of his "Mount Shasta" five years ago, his work to-day ought to be worth just as much and more. Therefore his placing a picture at auction of the same quality and quite as attractive a subject as others painted on commission, and allowing a competitive public to fix his price, is unjust to his art and places him in the annoying position of not being able to get any price that he himself sets."[159]

Among Hill's diverse offerings at the auction were both an oil sketch and a larger canvas of *South Dome, Yosemite*. These may be related to an engaging oil study of North Dome (fig. 60) that Hill organized into three receding planes, in keeping with Hudson River School practices. The brushwork is remarkably loose (note the marks defining the sharp boulders in the foreground), with the exception of the smoothly-painted sky. With fine effect, Hill exploits the contrast of tones between the deep browns and greens of the foreground and the cool gray granite in the distance. As in other compositions of single landmarks and unlike his broad vistas, Hill makes no reference to the human presence in this charming wilderness view.

RETURN TO YOSEMITE

Sometime in May 1882, Hill returned to Yosemite accompanied by one of his daughters. His stay, which extended into August, coincided with a visit to the valley by fellow artist Charles Dorman Robinson, who also hoped to attract the patronage of Yosemite tourists. Perhaps seeking to gain an edge over his Yosemite competitors, Hill made an application, approved by the Park Commissioners, to construct a studio "at a site to be selected."[160] Following his summer sojourn, Hill set up a studio in San Francisco, this time in the Mechanics' Library Building. In these quarters, he displayed his *The Driving of the Last Spike,* which he had retouched in areas, and proceeded to paint Yosemite scenes from sketches.

Hill remained a favorite of the press, which described him as "eminently a painter of California scenery, and his Yosemite works are better than anything he has done for several years." Yosemite's magnetic appeal probably led Hill to announce his intentions to construct a "comfortable cottage" (most likely the sanctioned studio) in Yosemite Valley the following summer and to paint another monumental canvas of that location. Yosemite was where he

FIGURE 60
Thomas Hill
North Dome, Yosemite Valley, ca. 1870.
Oil on paper mounted on board, 14 x 18 in.
Gibson, Dunn & Crutcher, Los Angeles.

FIGURE 61
Thomas Hill
Royal Arches and Half Dome, Yosemite, n.d.
Oil on paper mounted on board, 14 x 21 in.
Private collection.

hoped to "spend the remaining summers of his life. He will make studies of the valley at every point, and intends to centre his entire attention on the subject."[161]

These comments were made even as Hill was exhibiting landscape paintings of the Connecticut River developed from earlier sketches made in the East. His focus was hardly exclusively on Yosemite, and he depicted a variety of locations for many years to come. Yosemite did offer Hill a subject for which there was an enthusiastic audience, as well as a summer retreat from San Francisco that afforded some stability.

Hill's extended summer journeys throughout California, New England, and elsewhere, and his independent lifestyle contributed to (or were symptomatic of) his deteriorating relationship with his wife. The demands and tensions of raising a large family also may have contributed to a breakdown of their marriage, and by the early 1880s, the Hills were living apart. It is not surprising that Hill sought a place where he might find refuge during summers and at other times. Yosemite promised to meet both his personal and financial goals.

Hill apparently completed his studio structure at the east end of Yosemite Valley and continued making oil sketches of various sites during the summer of 1883. Few dated studies have come to light, challenging efforts to determine if Hill's style was evolving in these small works, or if he was continuing approaches he had developed during the previous decade. His practice of taking orders for paintings of subjects he had not visited for many years further complicates understanding of his work at this time.

Comparisons with large canvases (many of which are undated) suggest that sylvan scenes such as *Royal Arches and Half Dome* (fig. 61) or *Cascade Creek, Yosemite Valley* (fig. 62) were created in the 1870s, whereas less detailed, broader representations (e.g. *Vernal and Nevada Falls*, fig. 63), are products of the 1880s. It seems likely that peaceful high country subjects, among them *Crescent Lake, Yosemite* (see page 5) were painted in the late 1870s. Although *Royal Arches* was featured in a large-scale painting as early as 1873, the sketch *Royal Arches and Half Dome* is similar in many ways to Hill's canvas *Mist in Tenaya Canyon*, executed in 1885.

By early 1884, Hill had completed his large Yosemite painting, originally destined for the Marquis of Lorne, but sent to the Art Association's spring exhibition. Other works at this time included a number of portraits and a large cartoon of "Truth and Falsehood" for the annual Bohemian Club "high-jinks."

FIGURE 62
Thomas Hill
Cascade Creek, Yosemite Valley, ca. 1878.
Oil on canvas, 13 x 10 in.
Private collection.

FIGURE 63
Thomas Hill
Vernal and Nevada Falls, n.d.
Oil on board, 21 x 13 in.
Pittock Mansion Society, Portland, Oregon.

Purportedly busy with commissions for clients in the East, Hill was characterized as "well-to-do, though [he] has met with varying fortunes, ill health, and has a large family on his hands."[162]

As Hill was spending more time away from San Francisco, press attention to his activities diminished. When he arrived in Yosemite Valley in 1884, his newly-constructed studio had been demolished by a storm. Hill settled instead at Clark's Station, near Wawona. He cut his summer visit short that year, returning to San Francisco by mid-August.

YELLOWSTONE AND THE ROCKIES

Hill thereupon departed for Yellowstone National Park, "where several Eastern artists have gone before him, and, it is said, have made wonderful sketches."[163]

It was Hill's first exposure to the Western landscape that had brought Thomas Moran to national prominence some ten years earlier. Hill made a number of paintings of Yellowstone subjects, and seems to have spent several months in the area, where he "traveled altogether about four hundred miles by stage, and has reveled in canyon scenery, bear shooting, Indian fighting, and all the pleasures of the frontier."[164]

A compelling oil sketch of *Giant Geyser, Yellowstone* (fig. 64) and small paintings on canvas of the Grand Canyon of the Yellowstone were made at this time. Hill's depiction of an erupting geyser is consistent with his recent interest in presenting single landscape motifs prominently in the foreground. In contrast, his small oil of *Grand Canyon of the Yellowstone* (fig. 65) offers an awesome vista recorded with much greater detail, despite the large scale of its subject. This study, which sumptuously renders the marvelous cataract from near Artist's Point, closely resembles Moran's well-known canvas of this subject (fig. 66). Hill used it (or a similar study) for a large canvas himself, although few of his paintings of Yellowstone and its environs survive. Despite popular public interest in the area, Yellowstone's dramatic landscapes did not engage Hill's ongoing interest.

There is also evidence that Hill developed oil sketches as well as large canvases from the work of other artists and photographers. While *Grand Canyon of the Yellowstone*, reminiscent as it is of Moran, may have been created independently, Hill's oil sketch of another Western landmark made famous by that artist, *Mountain of the Holy Cross* (fig. 67), seems likely to be derived from another work (probably Moran's painting or survey photographs by William Henry Jackson). Not only was it quite difficult to view the cruciform pattern of snow, but there is no record that Hill visited this area.[165]

Upon returning to California late in 1884, Hill set to work at the studio he occupied at Clark's Station. There he quickly completed exhibition-size paintings of Yellowstone Canyon and Yosemite, which, with his *The Driving of the Last Spike*, were sent off in early December to be featured in the New

FIGURE 64
Thomas Hill
Giant Geyser, Yellowstone, n.d.
Oil on paper mounted on board,
20½ x 13¾ in.
Arthur J. Phelan, Jr.

Thomas Hill
Grand Canyon of the Yellowstone, ca. 1884.
Oil on canvas, 18 x 24 in.
Private collection.

Thomas Moran
(United States, 1837–1926)
The Grand Canyon of the Yellowstone, 1872.
Oil on canvas, 84 x 144 in.
National Museum of American Art,
Smithsonian Institution; lent by the U.S.
Department of the Interior, Office of the
Secretary.

Orleans World's Industrial and Cotton Exposition. The Yellowstone Canyon work was reviewed when Hill made a brief stop in San Francisco, and described as

> cover[ing] a good deal of canvas, and if it is the artist's intention to con-
> fuse the beholder by depicting a wild scene with wild colors, then he has
> certainly reached what he has striven for. Mr. Hill is one of the few Cali-
> fornians who have visited the scene, and the only one who has attempted
> to paint it. . . . Into the work Mr. Hill has thrown all his characteristic spirit
> as a landscape painter and as an artist who is not afraid to undertake any-
> thing. Where others would have trifled with the subject and treated it with
> a nicety of detail, he has stepped aside to boldly delineate the lights and
> shades and the dazzling colors of the scene.[166]

TRIP TO NEW ORLEANS

Hill seemed to be re-invigorated by his Yellowstone trip. In late November 1884 he was described as "looking better than for any time within the past two years." His activities in the following months demonstrated Hill's continued energy, as well as his interest in partaking of new experiences, maintaining his visibility, and exploring new avenues to promote his work.[167]

Within six weeks, by mid-January 1885, Hill was in Louisiana "making sketches on an old plantation on the Mississippi River, above New Orleans."[168]

No small paintings of the plantation have been identified or documented; it is unknown whether many Louisiana paintings were produced, and, if so, if the artist was satisfied with the results.

The Louisiana journey proved disappointing overall for Hill. The art exhibition, for which he assisted with the installation, failed to open on time, and one critic noted in late January that "The usual week or ten days yet is repeated with provoking regularity." Further, his contributions to the event received disparaging reviews in the East. *The Driving of the Last Spike* was severely criticized as "an arid picture without a shade of excuse for its being." While his Yellowstone and Yosemite paintings were cited for their impressive subjects, they fared little better, provoking the judgment that they were "instructive geologically, but their worth is not great." Despite these developments, Hill stayed on for some time, and although reported as "tiring of New Orleans" in late February, he did not return to San Francisco until nearly a month later.[169]

At Home in Wawona

Hill attended the wedding of his daughter Estella and John Washburn, a proprietor of Yosemite's Wawona Hotel, on April 28, 1885. The ceremony, at the "handsome" home in Oakland, was attended by a large number of people, most of whom were family members. One social column concluded with the report that: "At 3 o'clock, the newly wedded pair, accompanied by Mr. Thomas Hill, Mrs. Edward Hill and other members of the family started for Monterey, where they will remain for a few days and then go to Yosemite."[170]

From this time on, Hill found a haven at Wawona, where the Washburns provided him rooms and constructed a studio for him nearby (in 1886). In this environment, Hill worked and sold his paintings to Yosemite visitors. He was tended to by his daughter as well as by Willetta Hill. A gifted artist in her own right, Willetta was married to Hill's eldest son, Edward. She remained at Wawona after her divorce and became Hill's traveling companion during the latter years of his life. This relationship may have contributed to the disruption of Hill's own marriage and been a cause for him to disengage from activities in San Francisco.[171]

As late as August 1885, Hill was still contending with difficulties associated with the New Orleans Exposition, "where after many luxuriant promises he fared very badly, and, to add insult to injury, was compelled to pay heavy freight charges out of his own pocket in order to get his pictures back at all." Additionally, it was noted that "Hill is a good business man and an artist with a national reputation. Affairs must have been very badly managed when he has such a complaint to make."[172]

This setback may have led to the sale of Hill's commodious Seminary Avenue home, on which there was a large lien, at a loss in early 1886. Hill maintained studios in both San Francisco and Wawona, most of his children were maturing, and the large residence may have been a burden to his wife, who subsequently acquired a "homestead residence" in Oakland.[173] Hill also continued to lease his studio in Yosemite Valley in the late 1880s.[174]

According to records, Yosemite visitors were directed by the Washburns to the artist's nearby studio at Wawona, which was adorned from floor to ceiling with animal skins, Indian baskets, and Hill's paintings. Hill received and fulfilled a large number of orders from his quarters, as documented in an account book he maintained there between 1884 and 1887.

The 163 sales noted during this four-year period indicate that Hill was producing large numbers of Yosemite scenes in standard sizes upon request, probably ordered from oil sketches and other paintings at the studio (fig. 69). The request of William J. Parks of Hartford, Connecticut, for an *Early Morning,* "with more midday effect, more detail in El Capitan," offers insight into Hill's transactions.

His subjects ranged as far afield as Mount Rainier and Mount Shasta, but *Early Morning, General View, Bridal Veil Meadow,* and Bridal Veil, Nevada, Vernal, and Yosemite Falls were the most popular views. The preferred formats were sixteen by twenty-four inches, twenty-six by thirty-five inches, thirty by forty-five inches, thirty-six by sixty inches, and thirty-six by fifty-four inches. Prices ranged from $50 (for what appear to be sketches) to $500 (for larger canvases), and Hill forwarded paintings to the homes of purchasers when they were completed.

FIGURE 68
Thomas Hill
Yosemite, 1875.
Oil on panel, 11½ x 17½ in.
Leo and Florence Helzel.

Although Hill had several commissions from notable Northern Californians (among them Governor George Stoneman and John Muir), clients living nearby accounted for only 5 percent of the sales in his account book. His primary buyers were tourists from the East and Midwest, many from New York State and Massachusetts, as well as visitors from the British Empire, including residents of New Zealand, Australia, Bombay, and London.

Sales from his Yosemite studio alone (including oil sketches) earned Hill in excess of $8,500 annually in the years covered. His sales at Wawona were critical to his livelihood, and motivated Hill to rapidly produce a number of Yosemite views that are uninspired and unrepresentative of his true talent. Though they helped provide financial stability in his life, these routine canvases did little to impress critics in San Francisco and other art centers, from which he was already distanced.

While Hill was still painting other subjects for public exhibition, including views of Oregon, the *Headwaters of the Madison River,* and *Yellowstone Lake* he

showed at the Art Association, he was "fast becoming a painter of Yosemite." His growing association with Yosemite was acknowledged by one reviewer, who commented that "by his faithfulness to his subject he has almost made it his own, and no artist has yet been able to contend with him."[175]

VARIED SUBJECTS

Hill did not dedicate himself completely to Yosemite. When summoned to New England in the early summer of 1886 after the death of his parents within weeks of each other, Hill spent time painting with Champney in the White Mountains, which he claimed as "still mecca for landscape artists." And he contributed his *Grand Canyon of the Yellowstone* to the State Fair art exhibition that fall, listing himself as a resident of San Francisco, which underscored his continued interests there.[176]

Hill rented the rooms of the Art Association for another large public sale of his works, which was conducted by Easton and Eldridge, auctioneers, on December 22, 1886.[177] As in his two previous sales, nearly half of the offerings (201 total) were described as "sketches." Hill's remarks in his sales catalogue introduction were confined to the smaller oil sketches, for which he showed obvious affection:

> I feel it my duty to give some explanation of this wholesale slaughter of my original studies from nature, which I have prized above gold. For many years they have been like my children, dear companions, calling up some of the happiest days of my life, with its struggles and uncertainties."

To justify parting with these works, he proceeded to cite the difficulty of storing and insuring them.

Unlike the 1882 sale, many of the oil sketches apparently were exhibited unframed, but Hill framed all of his larger paintings and some of the sketches.

He guarded against losses by determining that the frames would be sold separately, at cost, to purchasers, and stated that "I shall deem it a personal favor if my choice of frame is accepted."[178]

Hill wrote that some of the oil sketches "date back thirty years." Since he had regularly included such works in large public sales since the mid-1870s, many of the studies were probably created within the two or three years preceding the auction. Others may have been offered at previous auctions, but had not sold. Fewer than a quarter of the sketches featured Yosemite motifs (despite the considerable time Hill had spent there), with New Hampshire and other California sites, including Mount Shasta and Lake Tahoe, prominently represented.

In contrast, more than a third of the "framed paintings" depicted Yosemite scenes. Subjects, however, varied from *Fort Dumpling, Newport, Rhode Island*; *Garden of the Gods, Colorado*; and *A Toiler in the New England Forest*; to *On Baldwin's Ranch, Los Angeles*; and *Cacti, from Nature*.

The sale generated "considerable interest in art circles," and the final sixty paintings "were quickly disposed of . . . at prices which were most satisfactory," but the $13,843 raised was comparable to the proceeds Hill had realized for fewer than half this number of works in his initial auction in 1874. The average purchase price of only $67 per piece was certainly a disappointment, and the highest selling painting (a large canvas of Yellowstone) went for only $800.

SCHOOL DIRECTOR

The event was likely an emotional one for Hill, whose longtime friend Virgil Williams had died suddenly only four days earlier. In the days before the sale, Hill served as a pallbearer at the funeral and volunteered to direct the School of Design, without compensation, until a replacement for Williams could be appointed.[179]

Hill undoubtedly made his generous offer to the School of Design out of his friendship for Williams and with optimism for the success of his upcoming sale. He began his interim duties almost immediately, but his lack of formal teaching and administrative experience proved a liability. Given his erratic participation in the affairs of the school over the years, Hill's abrupt departure in mid-March to travel to Alaska to make studies for a commission from John Muir, may not have been surprising to his longtime colleagues.[180]

The challenges the art school must have presented to someone of Hill's temperament were noted in the press as a mitigating factor:

> Who could expect the man who is accustomed to study nature in the grand wilds of the Yosemite to sit for several hours a day within the confines of four walls suggesting, correcting, guiding and instructing. And worse still, to have a dozen or more pupils lean over his work when he took the brush and ask why he used Naples yellow in place of yellow ochre, whey he put shades in one place and high lights in another, why he did not work his skies in with Prussian blue or indigo and his trees and grasses with chrome green, touching up the deep tones with asphaltum. . . . How could an artist who learned his lessons from nature in nature's

labyrinths answer a hundred and one technical questions? It is no wonder he burst the bonds and started for Alaska, to get away from the crippling restraint.[181]

PICTURESQUE CALIFORNIA

The allure of Alaska's stunning landscapes must have been overpowering to Hill, ever eager to travel and paint new scenes. There he made studies for a large canvas of Muir Glacier and for illustrations to be reproduced in the luxurious publication entitled *Picturesque California and the Region West of the Rockies from Alaska to Mexico.* Edited by Muir and issued in various formats in New York and San Francisco by J. Dewing and Company beginning in 1888, *Picturesque California* offered a significant commission as well as an excellent forum for Hill's work.

A number of artists including William Keith, Thomas Moran, Frederic Remington, Julian Walbridge Rix, and Charles Dorman Robinson produced

paintings and drawings for the 120 photogravures and etched plates that appeared throughout the text. Hill was prominently represented with eighteen views (including Yosemite motifs like *Two Guardsmen* (fig. 70) and *Chilnoolna Falls,* as well as subjects such as *Spearing Salmon* and *McCloud River Falls*). A number of smaller line drawings were also interspersed with the texts. With such a large number of pieces, he was one of the most visible contributors to the publication. Since his subjects were diverse geographically, it is uncertain whether Hill traveled to Southern California to undertake scenes of *Los Angeles* and *Palm Valley* that also appeared in the work.

A number of the paintings Hill submitted to be reproduced as photogravures for *Picturesque California* survive. These were likely created over a period of several months. Hill probably drew upon earlier sketches as the basis for most of the compositions, developing only a few new subjects in the field. Many of the sketches (e.g., *Two Guardsmen,* fig. 71) are *grisailles,* undertaken in various shades of gray ranging from almost white to near black. This medium would have allowed Hill to create the range of values needed for the images to be translated effectively in the print medium.

FIGURE 72
Thomas Hill
The Davidson Glacier, ca. 1888.
Oil on plywood, 14 x 21 in.
The Gilcrease Museum, Tulsa, Oklahoma.

FIGURE 73
Thomas Hill
"Davidson Glacier," from *Picturesque
California*, 1888.
Photogravure, 6½ x 9⅞ in.
California History Section, California
State Library, Sacramento.

Other sketches utilize color, with touches of sepia and cool blue tones. *The Davidson Glacier* (fig. 72) departs most dramatically from the monochromatic tonality of the other images. The freshness of this scene may reflect Hill's recent contact with the glacier and the impression that it and its awesome setting may have had on him. Like many of the artist's compositions, *The Davidson Glacier* is enlivened by figures; these are placed both on shore and in a boat whose diagonal wake provides an angle balancing that of the icefield. This sketch testifies that Hill's powers of observation remained strong (note the interplay of the smooth water and colorful shore with the sheaves of ice descending the slope), and his ability to convey complex forms with painterly "notations" had not abated.

As was his custom, Hill drew upon his experiences in Alaska to create oil sketches for some time afterward. Two examples are similar views of the Inland Passage, one of which is dated 1886, but probably comes from the following year (fig. 74). The second, undated view, is embellished with two boats containing fishermen (fig. 75), and rendered from a point not far from the vantage of the first sketch. The works, however, differ in both atmospheric effect and in the prominence given to the soaring mountain peak.

FIGURE 76
Thomas Hill
Alaska Scene near Juneau, 1894.
Oil on paper, 14 x 20¾ in.
Private collection.

Significantly, the undated version reveals a *pentimento* in the sky at the upper right, a rarity in Hill's oil sketches. Since the artist must have been painting aboard ship (if these scenes were directly observed), he may have had to respond to an unanticipated shift in position, or perhaps the original placement of the mountain further to the right proved unsatisfactory.

In *Alaska Scene near Juneau* of 1894 (fig. 76), Hill gives even greater emphasis to the ephemeral effect created by both the floating fog and the water that comprises the foreground.

Picturesque California and another publication titled *In the Heart of the Sierras* (published in 1886 by James Mason Hutchings with a number of drawings "contributed" by Hill) brought the artist renewed public attention. But in the late 1880s Hill was in residence at Wawona, and, despite exhibiting and winning premiums at the Mechanics' Institute, the California State Fair, and national exhibitions, his activities were recorded only sporadically in San Francisco papers.

TRAVELS FROM WAWONA

Nearly sixty years old, the gregarious artist had largely retreated to Yosemite, where he entertained visitors and accepted orders for paintings. Visits to San Francisco and other destinations including Monterey and San Diego were special occasions. He continued to produce many paintings of high accomplishment based on a mature style that had been refined for some time. Instead of experimenting with new methods during these years, Hill undertook work characterized by continuity and a return to familiar subjects. As one observer commented, Hill "sticks to his characteristic style of work. . . . He sees things that way, and paints them that way, and certainly deserves credit for having faith in his convictions."[182]

Thomas Hill's stature in the art world (as well as the importance of his oil sketches to him) were acknowledged in a profile of the day:

> Tom Hill is one of the best known landscape artists in California, and has a well-recognized position which time has not materially altered. He is the man of the world of the profession. Shrewd, yet kindly, perfectly alive to the money-making side of his work, yet a thoroughgoing artist as regards ability and knowledge of the requirements. If Hill does not do better work it is because of his skepticism in regard to public taste and certain limitations natural to the man. There is not the slightest touch of improvidence about him and he is without petty jealousy or small fear of the merits of others. He is a man of plain manners and full of plain surroundings. His rooms on Stockton street are his studio. There are no draperies, no accessories . . . from India, China, Egypt or Italy. The sketch made in the Sierras, or in the Yosemite, or else again on the great waters of Lake George, lies on his easel. This he perfects as much as possible without entirely destroying the spirit and freshness of the original. Almost an impossible task. But the public will not have sketches and effects. They want detail, finished pictures, and, as the sagacious artist before quoted says, "It takes money to paint." Hill has a fund of reminiscences about the grub-street side of San Francisco artist life. He has wide sympathy, indeed a profound respect, for those of his brethren who despise money and dare to throw it away, but he is not one of that kind himself, not by any means.[183]

Though contemporary commentaries on Hill's personality and lifestyle differed significantly, there was general agreement on his generosity and his fondness for and rapport with children. He enjoyed cigars, and had a billiards table in the room adjacent to his display gallery at Wawona. To satisfy his hunger for quail (his dinner two or three times each week), Hill hired young Jay Bruce to hunt for him in 1894 and provided the boy with a rifle and ammunition.[184] In contrast to the austerity of Hill's studio in San Francisco, his Wawona quarters were richly furnished (fig. 77), and Hill's earnings from his sales to tourists appear to have allowed him to live comfortably in his later years.

Hill continued to travel throughout the 1890s, and patronized San Francisco's Palace Hotel, the Hotel del Coronado in San Diego, and other eminent establishments, insofar as his health permitted. He painted in the White Mountains during the summer of 1892, and despite an apparent medical crisis in January 1893, traveled by rail to Chicago that fall to attend the World's Columbian Exposition.[185] There his work was featured in the California section organized by fellow artist Norton Bush. Hill contributed a triptych of *Wawona* flanked by panels showing giant sequoias, and paintings of Yosemite Valley, *California, A Scene near Los Gatos, Muir Glacier* and *The Driving of the Last Spike* (the final two being large canvases). With the exception of the view near Los Gatos, all of the works were lent by the artist.[186]

Although Hill expressed his interest in settling in San Francisco upon his return via Washington and Oregon, he was not active there. During the summer of 1894 he was again at Wawona experiencing continued infirmity, though it was noted that "his health has not prevented his working, and he has made a number of characteristic sketches as well as doing considerable work on several larger pictures."[187]

PAINTING OUTDOORS IN CALIFORNIA

The custom of regularly painting in the field on sketching expeditions had become deeply ingrained in California painters by 1894, with the *Call* observing that

> For the past two months, most of the studios of the city have been closed, while artists have been at work out of doors. Some have spent the summer among the mountains while others have gone to the seaside or up among the redwoods. . . .
>
> The result as shown by the large numbers of sketches brought back is most encouraging. It shows that the artists have studied conscientiously and endeavored to obtain truth rather than mere pictorial effect. Some of the artists have brought back dozens of small sketches, while others devoted their time to rather fair-sized canvases.[188]

Even if Northern Californian artists were isolated from the European modernist experiments and from interchange with many leading American painters of the day, they were experienced as painters of the out-of-doors. The magnificent landscape vistas to which they had immediate access both inhibited and inspired their efforts, for such grand scenes begged to be recorded more than reflected upon or transformed. This was the challenge for Albert Bierstadt, Thomas Moran, and other Western artists as well.

At the same time, the freshly-observed oil sketches by Hill and his colleagues informed the exquisite California watercolors of artists such as Christian Jorgensen (fig. 78) and Lorenzo Latimer. They also served as precursors to the engaging small-format paintings made directly from the landscape by San Francisco's first generation of modernist painters, The Society of Six.

In 1894, Hill donated a large painting of the Rio Grande, the canvas surrounded by "a unique frame, made by himself from wood obtained from some of the great trees at the Mariposa Grove," to the Press Club.[189] Whether Hill actually visited the Rio Grande is subject to speculation, as over the years he used whatever resources were available to him to compose paintings, from photographs and schematic pencil sketches (fig. 79) to oil sketches. Further, his oil sketches consistently functioned in a variety of ways; they served as studies for larger compositions, acted as models from which patrons might order, and evolved as fully-realized paintings in their own rights (fig. 80).

FIGURE 78
Christian Jorgensen
(United States, 1860–1935)
Happy Isles, 1906.
Watercolor on paper, 11½ x 10 in.
Crocker Art Museum.

FIGURE 79
Thomas Hill
Royal Arch Lake, n.d.
Pencil on paper, 5½ x 15 in.
Crocker Art Museum.

FIGURE 80
Thomas Hill
Valley with Deer, n.d.
Oil on paper mounted on board, 12 x 18 in.
William A. Karges.

THE ARTIST/PROMOTER

When opportunities presented, Hill eagerly promoted his paintings in a manner not dissimilar to that of the showmen of the West. Lady Theodora Guest recounted her visit to Hill's Studio and the colorful exhibits there in *A Round Trip in North America,* published in 1895:

> After supper we were conducted to the studio of a painter—one Mr. Hill, who had made some effective pictures of Yo Semite, chiefly from one point of view . . . He had various curiosities hung around his studio—wasp nests, hideously large, dead rattlesnakes, skins of coyote, squirrels, and wildcats.

Guest closed her comments by noting that "from a business standpoint Hill's Wawona studio was ideally located and commanded the attention of the 'cream' of tourist travel."[190] Although Hill reportedly sold only art work and pressed flowers for the ladies from his Wawona studio, Jay Bruce recalled supplying the artist with rattlesnake skins for sale as souvenirs.[191] It is likely that trophies, Indian baskets, and other Western items adorning his establishment were also for sale.

Hill continued to attract notice in newspaper accounts generated on his returns to San Francisco. When he passed through for one day before departing for Victoria, the *San Francisco Call* of December 5, 1895 proclaimed:

Artist Tom Hill Is Back
He Is En Route to Mount Baker to Paint It for a London Banker
A BUSY SEASON FOR HIM
Has Sold Over $10,000 Worth of Pictures Besides
the Big One of Yosemite

A $5,000 commission was referenced twice in the accompanying article, as were Hill's hopes to exhibit his paintings at the Royal Academy in London. There was even talk that Princess Louise, Queen Victoria's daughter and an English representative in Western Canada, had asked him to paint a Canadian scene for her.[192] It is not likely that Hill realized these projects, as his trip was cut short after he and his party encountered harsh weather in Oregon and decided to return to San Francisco.[193]

Although Princess Louise's entreaty was apparently never fulfilled, Hill produced several sketches of Bow River Gap (fig. 81), near Banff. When he had traveled there is uncertain, however. A study formerly in the collection of Dunbarton Oaks bears the inscription "Original Sketch/of Bow River Gap, at Banff, on/Canadian Pacific R.R./Painted by T. Hill" on its reverse, implying that Hill did visit that area in the course of his extensive travels.

FIGURE 81
Thomas Hill
Bow River Gap at Banff, on Canadian Pacific Railroad, n.d.
Oil on canvas, 13¾ x 21 in.
Dr. Oscar and Trudy Lemer.

A CAREER DECLINES

Hill probably spent the remainder of the winter of 1895–96 in Yosemite, and the following summer he suffered the first of a series of strokes while at Wawona. Although he continued to visit San Francisco periodically and new paintings were noted, his production diminished, and articles on his accomplishments adopted a retrospective tenor.[194] Still, as late as 1899, his Yosemite studio remained a center of activity with Hill "at home each evening to visitors from the big hotel and there is seldom one who does not visit his studio. It is an art exhibition which goes on continuously, with a steady stream of visitors constantly coming and going."[195]

A second account book, with entries dating from 1896 to 1900, shows that sales had slowed. Nevertheless, the erratic notations indicate that Hill earned over $2,000 from sales of his artwork in March of 1896. As before, his patrons were predominantly from outside California and desirous of Yosemite views. In addition, two depictions of Selkirk Glacier, a Mount Hood, and a Bow River Gap sketch were also among Hill's sales that year.[196]

At the end of 1896, Hill and Willetta departed for Mexico in search of a better climate. Frustrated in their quest, they settled in at Coronado in Southern California for over two months, then returned via Los Angeles, Santa Barbara, and Carmel.[197] Several oil sketches of Mexico in Hill's estate were likely created at this time. Accounts indicate that Hill was installed at Wawona again by April and continuing to accept orders for representative Yosemite scenes. By 1898, he also was selling work at Coronado, where he reputedly conducted an active business as well. Hill returned there during the winters of 1899 and 1902, and possibly at other times.[198]

Hill's national standing was confirmed when President Theodore Roosevelt requested a tour of the Wawona studio during his visit to Yosemite in 1903. The artist of course complied, and presented the president with a view of Bridal Veil Falls he had admired. Hill was, however, in failing health, and required "constant care" at Wawona and his winter cottage in nearby Raymond. As late as 1906, he was recorded as "still at work and his easel is set up at a very early hour each morning,"[199] and it is likely that he continued to paint throughout the months preceding his death on June 30, 1908.

REMEMBERING A PATHFINDER

Although Hill was eulogized at length in both the New York and San Francisco papers, his obituaries were primarily biographical, citing honors and awards, yet failing to note the artist's larger contributions. The professional accomplishments and energy that Hill brought to the nascent art community in California in the 1860s and 1870s provided needed stature and credibility at a critical time in its development. Unlike Bierstadt, Moran, and others who came as visitors, Hill was a resident artist (both in "boom" times and through economic adversity), who offered leadership and hospitality to his colleagues.

By the time of his death, Hill's finest paintings represented the vision of an earlier generation. But in the 1860s and 1870s he had been instrumental in defining an aesthetic for depicting California and broader American landscapes, as much in his small paintings (the oil sketches) as in his large-scale

representations. With their immediacy of impact and understanding of nature, Hill's images uniquely reference the character of his era and the American landscape experience.

Two years after Hill's death, an admiring tribute to his life work appeared in *The Argonaut:*

> The recent death of Thomas Hill, the landscape painter, was one of the closing events, it is felt by California artists, of an important epoch in the development of things artistic in this State. He was one of the first to make the world at large realize, forty or fifty years ago, that on this western coast—generally regarded as a region somewhat beyond the bounds of civilization, where comfortable fortunes were uncomfortably made—there were men who painted pictures that were worth considering. Hill was, in fact, one of the "pathfinders" for those artists who have since won fame for themselves by sending out pictures exploiting the beauties of California.[200]

1. To date, the most substantial publication on the artist is Marjorie Dakin Arkelian's *Thomas Hill: The Grand View* (Oakland, Calif.: The Oakland Museum, 1980), published in conjunction with an exhibition at the museum. Other titles that address Hill's work include Birgitta Hjalmarson, "Thomas Hill," *Antiques* 126 (November 1984): 1200–1207; Kate Nearpass Ogden, "Sublime Vistas and Scenic Backdrops: Nineteenth-Century Painters and Photographers at Yosemite," *California History* 69 (Summer 1990): 134–153 and "God's Great Plow and the Scripture of Nature, Art and Geology at Yosemite," *California History* 71 (Spring 1992): 88–109; and Janice Driesbach, *Bountiful Harvest: 19th-Century California Still Life Painting* (Sacramento, Calif.: Crocker Art Museum, 1991).

2. Hill's activities and his contributions to exhibitions were regularly noted in San Francisco newspapers and journals from 1872 through the late 1880s. Such publications included the *California Art Gallery, Daily Alta California, Daily Evening Post, Evening Bulletin, San Francisco News Letter and California Advertiser,* and *San Francisco Chronicle.* Catalogues from Hill's 1886 auction and from estate sales organized in both 1908 and 1910, along with two of his account books, are in the collection of the Crocker Art Museum.

3. This number is based on information available from the Inventory of American Paintings compiled by the National Museum of American Art, Smithsonian Institution, from museum and private collection surveys, and from files maintained by early California painting dealers and collectors.

4. Marjorie Dakin Arkelian, *Thomas Hill: The Grand View* (Oakland, Calif.: The Oakland Museum, 1980), 10–11. This publication, which draws extensively upon Hill family archives and information from members of the family, is the primary source on Hill's early years.

5. Ruth N. Post, "Virgil Macey Williams, 1830–1886" (Crocker Art Museum Archives, n.d., typescript), 15–16. This document provides excellent biographical information about Williams and his associates.

6. Though Hill family records provide considerable information, a number of significant dates are either absent or inconsistent with Hill's ventures as reported in contemporary press accounts.

7. Robert H. Fletcher, "Memorandum of Artists" (San Francisco Art Association Records, 1906, typescript), 3, cited in Arkelian, *Thomas Hill,* 11. This document is available at the California State Library. As Arkelian notes, there are no surviving records at the Pennsylvania Academy of Fine Arts indicating that Hill paid tuition there.

8. Fletcher, "Memorandum of Artists," 3.

9. Fletcher, "Memorandum of Artists," 3.

10. Benjamin Champney, *Sixty Years' Memories of Art and Artists* (Woburn, Mass.: The News Print, Wallace and Andrew, 1900).

11. *Boston Evening Transcript,* 21 June 1858.

12. Nancy K. Anderson and Linda S. Ferber, *Albert Bierstadt: Art and Enterprise* (Brooklyn: The Brooklyn Museum in association with Hudson Hills Press, 1990), 140.

13. Arkelian, *Thomas Hill,* 12; she refers to a letter dated April 13, 1861 from the artist's cousin Benjamin Hill to relatives in England that reads in part: "Tom has gone to California because he thinks he can do better there and his health is not very good."

14. Langley, Henry G., comp., *The San Francisco Directory* (San Francisco: Valentine & Co., 1861), 179; and Langley, Henry G., comp., *San Fancisco Directory and Business Guide, 1862–63* (San Francisco: n.p., n.d.), 199.

15. Moreland Stevens, *Charles Christian Nahl: Artist of the Gold Rush* (Sacramento, Calif.: Crocker Art Gallery, 1976), 63–75; Post, "Virgil Williams"; and Peter Palmquist, *Carleton E. Watkins: Photographer of the American West* (Albuquerque, N.M.: University of New Mexico Press for the Amon Carter Museum, 1983), 199.

16. *Daily Alta California* (San Francisco), 13 July 1863.

17. *Evening Bulletin* (San Francisco), 26 August 1864.

18. Despite references to the effect that Hill traveled to Yosemite in 1862, there are no extant paintings or documents to establish that Hill visited there prior to 1865. Contemporary accounts document statements by Hill that he had been to Yosemite earlier, but in testimony in 1889, presumably given under oath, his response to the question "When were you there [in Yosemite]?" was "Every year for five or six years past . . . and have been going, as I told you for twenty-four years" (or since 1865). California Legislature, Assembly Committee on Yosemite Valley and Mariposa Grove of Big Trees, *In the Matter of the Investigation of the Yosemite Valley Commissioners*, in *Appendix to the Journals of the Senate and Assembly of the Twenty-Eighth Session of the Legislature of the State of California*, Vol. VIII (Sacramento, 1889), 428. Also Hardy Sloan George, "Thomas Hill: 1829–1908" (master's thesis, University of California at Los Angeles, 1963), p. 26; he cites "Report of the Fourth Industrial Exhibition of the Mechanics' Institute" (San Francisco: n.p., 1864), 39.

19. *Evening Bulletin* (San Francisco), 21 April 1865.

20. *Evening Bulletin* (San Francisco), 23 March 1865.

21. See "Chronology and Color Plates" in Anderson and Ferber, *Albert Bierstadt*, 173.

22. Anderson and Ferber, *Albert Bierstadt*, 201.

23. *Evening Bulletin* (San Francisco), 23 August 1865.

24. *Daily Alta California* (San Francisco), 10 October 1865.

25. The California Art Union was modelled on similar organizations that were founded in Europe and the East earlier in the century. It sought to cultivate public interest in art by "maintaining a gallery and making an annual distribution of works of art among its members." Such distributions were commonly prints made from art work purchased from regularly-scheduled exhibitions and allocated to subscribers, who paid a modest fee for this benefit, as well as original art work disbursed by lottery. See *A Classified Catalogue of the Paintings on Exhibition at the Room of the California Art Union with the Constitution and By-Laws and List of Officers* (San Francisco: The Art Union, 1865). Despite its intentions, the California Art Union apparently failed to distribute reproductions of Hill's *Merchant of Venice*.

26. *Evening Bulletin* (San Francisco), 11 November 1865.

27. A list of the paintings that Hill was exhibiting appeared in the *Evening Bulletin* (San Francisco) on 8 December 1865. No accounts of Hill traveling to the Northwest prior to that time have been located. Whether he visited these sites or relied on photographs and other images for his representations cannot be ascertained; his activities were recorded only sporadically in the local press during the 1860s.

28. Carol Troyen, "Innocents Abroad: American Painters at the 1867 Exposition Universelle, Paris," *American Art Journal* 16 (Fall 1984): 2. Family records and later accounts by Hill, the only sources of information on the artist's departure, do not indicate when he left California or arrived in Europe. His passport application, made in Dutchess County on 2 July 1866, is on file at the National Archives.

29. *Boston Evening Transcript*, 24 February 1868. An article indicates that Hill exhibited at the Exposition Universelle, stating that "at the French Exposition of last year no pictures by Americans were more favorably received," and adding that "Bowles & Drevet besought the exclusive sale of them. Andre Leo was very enthusiastic in their praise, and Couture, the artist, was sounding it in everyone's ear." However, as his name is absent from the checklist and written descriptions of that show, it seems unlikely Hill participated in the prestigious exhibition. Further, its East Coast organizing committee admitted only eighty-two pieces, practically all by artists working in New York City. Troyen, "Innocents Abroad," 4, 5, 25.

30. Troyen, "Innocents Abroad," 13, also 4, 18, 19, 25; she cites M. D. Conway, "The Great Show at Paris," *Harper's New Monthly Magazine* 35 (July 1867): 248.

31. Rudolf M. Bisanz, *The René von Schleinitz Collection of the Milwaukee Art Center: Major Schools of German Nineteenth-Century Popular Painting* (Milwaukee: Milwaukee Art Center, 1980), 183.

32. Watkins's photograph appears as "Plate 10" in his album, *Yosemite Valley: Photographic Views, Falls and Valley Yo-Semite in Mariposa County*, published in San Francisco in 1863.

33. *Boston Evening Transcript,* 14 May 1867; *The Evening Post* (New York), June 29 June 1867; and *Boston Business Directory,* 1868.

34. *Boston Evening Transcript,* 24 February 1868.

35. *Boston Post,* 13 June 1868.

36. *Boston Evening Transcript,* 17 June 1868.

37. See note 29 above; also *Boston Evening Transcript,* 17 June 1868.

38. *Boston Evening Transcript,* 17 June 1868, and *San Francisco News Letter and California Advertiser,* 22 January 1876.

39. Benjamin Parke Avery, "Art Beginnings on the Pacific," *Overland Monthly* 1 (August 1868): 113, and *San Francisco News Letter and California Advertiser,* 14 August 1869.

40. Anthony F. Janson, *Worthington Whittredge* (Cambridge: Cambridge University Press, 1989), 95.

41. *The Evening Post* (New York), 2 July 1868; *Boston Evening Tribune,* 3 November 1868 and 10 November 1868; and *The Evening Post* (New York), 18 December 1868.

42. Charles H. Brainard, "The Early Home of Whittier," *The Ramrod,* June 1869.

43. *Prang's Christmas Chromo* (Boston: Prang and Co., 1871); Larry Freeman, *Louis Prang, Color Lithographer: Giant of a Man* (Watkins Glen, N.Y.: Century House, n.d.), 63; and Katharine Morrison McClinton, *The Chromolithographs of Louis Prang* (New York: Clarkson N. Potter, 1973), 187, 194.

44. *Daily Evening Transcript* (Boston), 16 October 1869 and 4 December 1869.

45. Champney, *Sixty Years' Memories,* 145–46.

46. *Watson's Art Journal* (New York), 10 July 1869.

47. Hill exhibited a Yosemite painting at Jones & Wooll's in November 1868 (*Evening Bulletin* [San Francisco], 16 November 1868), and in April 1869, was represented in an exhibition at Snow & Roos Art Gallery with *On the Yuba River* and *Table Mountain* (exhibition catalogue, nos. 79 and 84). In January 1870 a twelve-by-twenty-inch sketch entitled *The Overhanging Tree* was described by the *San Francisco Call* (8 January 1870) while on view at Barry & Patten, and the following month Hill sent another four paintings to be shown in that city (*Evening Bulletin* [San Francisco], 16 February 1870). The *Evening Bulletin* (San Francisco) on 10 April 1869 recorded reports of the artist's impending return.

48. *Boston Evening Transcript,* 7 December 1870, and *Evening Bulletin* (San Francisco), 14 January 1871.

49. Edward Bosqui, *Memoirs of Edward Bosqui* (Oakland, Calif.: Holmes Book Company, 1952): 115–16, and *San Francisco News Letter and California Advertiser,* 25 March 1871. The *San Francisco News Letter and California Advertiser* (7 April 1877) also asserts that "If Mr. Hill had been here at the organization of the Association he would doubtless have been in favor of the 'Art Union principle,'" indicating that he had not been in California at the time of its organization.

50. Minutes of the San Francisco Art Association, 2 November 1871, Archives of American Art, roll 1288, and *Boston Evening Transcript,* 27 December 1871.

51. *Boston Evening Transcript,* 18 November 1871.

52. *Watson's Art Journal* (New York), 27 January 1872.

53. *Watson's Art Journal* (New York), 16 March 1872.

54. *Boston Evening Transcript,* 20 March 1872. It reports that "Tom Hill will soon make a trip to California, on a visit to Virgil Williams, who is living on a ranch near San Francisco. His friends hope he will recover his health in that genial climate."

55. *Evening Bulletin* (San Francisco), 2 May 1872.

56. *Evening Bulletin* (San Francisco), 29 May 1872.

57. *San Francisco News Letter and California Advertiser,* 8 June 1872. The Yosemite painting purchased by Charles Crocker was destroyed in the 1906 San Francisco earthquake and fire. Thus we must rely on the Prang chromolithograph and existing photographs to determine its appearance.

58. *Evening Bulletin* (San Francisco), 29 May 1872.

59. *Evening Bulletin* (San Francisco), 28 September 1872. The article suggests the regard in which Hill was held when it asserts that: "His presence and work cannot but have a good effect on local art."

60. *Evening Bulletin* (San Francisco), 9 November 1872 and 14 November 1872. Additionally, Hill donated photographs of fifteen of his paintings to the Arriola benefit.

61. *The Grizzly* (San Francisco), 14 December 1872.

62. *Evening Bulletin* (San Francisco), 27 January 1873.

63. *Boston Evening Transcript,* 21 February 1873.

64. *California Art Gallery* (San Francisco), March 1873.

65. *California Art Gallery* (San Francisco), April 1873.

66. *California Art Gallery* (San Francisco), May 1873.

67. *Evening Bulletin* (San Francisco), 21 May 1873, and *California Art Gallery* (San Francisco), May 1873.

68. *California Art Gallery* (San Francisco), April and July 1873.

69. *San Francisco News Letter and California Advertiser,* 23 August 1873.

70. *San Francisco News Letter and California Advertiser,* 23 August 1873.

71. *San Francisco News Letter and California Advertiser,* 27 September 1873.

72. *San Francisco News Letter and California Advertiser,* 4 October 1873.

73. *San Francisco News Letter and California Advertiser,* 1 November 1873.

74. *San Francisco News Letter and California Advertiser,* 25 October 1873.

75. *San Francisco News Letter and California Advertiser,* 1 November 1873; 15 November 1873; and 22 November 1873. See also "Art Notes," *Overland Monthly* 11 (November 1873): 477.

76. Minutes of the San Francisco Art Association, 22 December 1873, and Minutes of the California School of Design, 29 December 1873, Archives of American Art, roll 1288.

77. "Art Notes," *Overland Monthly* 12 (March 1874): 288.

78. *Daily Evening Post* (San Francisco), 6 February 1874.

79. *San Francisco News Letter and California Advertiser,* 21 March 1874.

80. *Illustrated Press* (San Francisco), April 1874. A model for this event was an auction sale, also primarily oil sketches, held by Edwin Deakin in May 1873. That sale, in contrast to Hill's offering, attracted little press attention, and its success is not documented. *Evening Bulletin* (San Francisco), 20 May 1873.

81. *Illustrated Press* (San Francisco), April 1874.

82. *San Francisco News Letter and California Advertiser,* 18 April 1874, and *Daily Alta California* (San Francisco), 20 April 1874.

83. *Daily Alta California* (San Francisco), 22 April 1874.

84. *Daily Evening Post* (San Francisco), 22 April 1874; *San Francisco News Letter and California Advertiser,* 25 April 1874; and "Art Notes," *Overland Monthly* 12 (June 1874).

85. *San Francisco News Letter and California Advertiser,* 11 July 1874 and 1 August 1874.

86. *Daily Evening Post* (San Francisco), 2 September 1874, and *San Francisco Call,* 20 September 1874.

87. *San Francisco Art Letter and California Advertiser,* 26 September 1874.

88. *Illustrated Press* (San Francisco), October 1874, and *San Francisco News Letter and California Advertiser,* 31 October 1874; 28 November 1874; and 20 February 1875.

89. *Evening Bulletin* (San Francisco), 25 January 1875.

90. *San Francisco News Letter and California Advertiser,* 20 February 1875.

91. *San Francisco News Letter and California Advertiser,* 10 April 1875 and 17 April 1875.

92. *San Francisco News Letter and California Advertiser,* 6 April 1875; 15 May 1875; 22 May 1875; and 5 June 1875, and *Boston Evening Tribune,* 22 June 1875.

93. As early as 22 May 1875, the *San Francisco News Letter and California Advertiser* reported that "It was expected that the picture of 'Driving the Last Spike,' of which we have heard so much the past year, and which, it was said, Mr. Hill had received a commission to paint, would be finished about now, and ready for exhibition . . . and just as we are on the tip-toe of expectation, it turns out that the picture is not now being, probably never will be, painted at all . . . and all this time our artist was reckoning without his host—he thought that his wished-for patron might possibly be as egotistical as himself, and that he would not refuse to purchase a painting intended to give him historical immortality. Such a reckoning would seem just on the part of a great artist, and there would seem to be no need of ordinary or extraordinary fawning. We sadly write, however, that we have the best authority for saying, no such commission has ever been given, or will be given, by Mr. Stanford—has in fact been refused. . . . Now, if all the commissions so much boasted of are of the same material, is it any wonder that the filling of them is put off, and strict attention given to painting pictures by the tens and hundreds for the auction room?"

94. *San Francisco News Letter and California Advertiser,* 5 June 1875.

95. *Boston Evening Transcript,* 2 July 1875.

96. Janson, *Worthington Whittredge,* 145. Also see Edward H. Dwight, *Worthington Whittredge (1820–1910): A Retrospective Exhibition of an American Artist* (Utica, N.Y.: Munson-Williams-Proctor Institute, 1969), which reproduces a drawing and an oil sketch by Whittredge of fellow artists painting *en plein air.* Anderson and Ferber, *Albert Bierstadt,* 192, 193.

97. *San Francisco News Letter and California Advertiser,* 31 July 1875.

98. His small painting of *Moonlight Trout Fishing* realized seventy-two dollars. A reader contested whether larger paintings, reported to have fetched from between four hundred and eight hundred dollars, had indeed been sold at all. *Daily Evening Post* (San Francisco), 24 November 1875, and *San Francisco News Letter and California Advertiser,* 27 November 1875. Nancy K. Anderson brought the parallel to Bierstadt's painting to my attention.

99. *Daily Alta California* (San Francisco), 7 November 1875, and *San Francisco News Letter and California Advertiser,* 22 January 1876.

100. *Daily Alta California* (San Francisco), 6 January 1876.

101. *San Francisco News Letter and California Advertiser,* 15 January 1876.

102. *Daily Alta California* (San Francisco), 7 November 1875, and *San Francisco News Letter and California Advertiser,* 22 January 1876.

103. *San Francisco News Letter and California Advertiser,* 8 January 1876; it included additional comments that "for this reason we suppose the picture of the 'Last Spike' was never painted. Figure painting is much more laborious than any other; more exacting in its details, for a landscapist can essay the fantastical."

104. *San Francisco News Letter and California Advertiser,* 19 February 1876.

105. *San Francisco News Letter and California Advertiser,* 27 May 1876.

106. *San Francisco News Letter and California Advertiser,* 29 July 1876, and *San Francisco Chronicle,* 11 September 1876.

107.   *San Francisco News Letter and California Advertiser*, 19 August 1876.

108.   There is correspondence in the archives of the Oakland Museum of California describing an oil sketch of Royal Arches that is inscribed "Santa Cruz" on the verso. Hill's account book from the 1890s, in the Crocker Art Museum collection, indicates that he was producing small format paintings of subjects encountered much earlier.

109.   *San Francisco News Letter and California Advertiser*, 11 November 1876 and 2 December 1876.

110.   B. E. Lloyd, *Lights and Shades in San Francisco* (San Francisco: A. L. Bancroft & Co., 1876), 416.

111.   *San Francisco News Letter and California Advertiser*, 27 January 1877.

112.   *San Francisco News Letter and California Advertiser*, 7 April 1877.

113.   *Daily Alta California* (San Francisco), 15 April 1877.

114.   *Daily Evening Post* (San Francisco), 14 April 1877; *San Francisco News Letter and California Advertiser*, 14 April 1877, 15 April 1877, and 21 April 1877; *Daily Alta California* (San Francisco), 19 April 1877.

115.   Minutes of the San Francisco Art Association, 3 May 1877, 16 May 1877, and 19 May 1877, Archives of American Art, roll 1288.

116.   *San Francisco Chronicle*, 3 June 1877; *San Francisco News Letter and California Advertiser*, 9 June 1877; and *Marin Journal* 7 June 1877.

117.   *San Francisco News Letter and California Advertiser*, 3 June 1877.

118.   *San Francisco Chronicle*, 29 July 1877 and *San Francisco News Letter and California Advertiser*, 4 August 1877, 13.

119.   *Boston Evening Transcript*, 14 May 1874.

120.   Although the eleven paintings that were lost were mostly Yosemite scenes and all by Hill, Gideon Jacques Denny was also asked to contribute replacement compositions, some of other California subjects. *San Francisco Bulletin*, 4 August 1877.

121.   *Daily Evening Post* (San Francisco), 15 September 1877, and *San Francisco News Letter and California Advertiser*, 29 September 1877.

122.   He was unsuccessful, as William Keith apparently took advantage of this situation to capture the prize, with Hill once again disparaged in the press. *San Francisco News Letter and California Advertiser*, 8 September 1877 and 29 September 1877.

123.   *San Francisco Chronicle*, 30 September 1877 and 21 October 1877; *San Francisco News Letter and California Advertiser*, 20 October 1877; *The Portico*, 3 November 1877 and 17 November 1877.

124.   *San Francisco News Letter and California Advertiser*, 22 December 1877.

125.   *San Francisco News Letter and California Advertiser*, 22 December 1877.

126.   *San Francisco News Letter and California Advertiser*, 26 January 1878.

127.   *San Francisco News Letter and California Advertiser*, 26 January 1878.

128.   *Daily Evening Post* (San Francisco), 13 April 1878, and *San Francisco Chronicle*, 14 April 1878, 28 April 1878, and 23 June 1878.

129.   *San Francisco Chronicle*, 8 December 1878.

130.   *San Francisco News Letter and California Advertiser*, 5 October 1878.

131.   *Pacific Coast Annual Mining Review*, (San Francisco: Francis & Valentine, 1878), 68.

132.   *San Francisco News Letter and California Advertiser*, 21 December 1878.

133.   Arkelian, *Thomas Hill*, 28.

134.   *San Francisco Evening Post*, 8 March 1879, and *The Argonaut*, 15 March 1879.

135.   *Daily Evening Post* (San Francisco), 17 May 1879.

136. *San Francisco Chronicle*, 11 May 1879; Hopps is also mentioned as a student of Hill in 1882. *Daily Evening Post* (San Francisco), 27 November 1882.

137. The mill, constructed by Samuel Taylor, at one time met the needs of three of San Francisco's evening newspapers. It was supplied by rags and scrap paper collected in San Francisco and sorted by low-paid Chinese laborers. Lincoln Fairly, "Mt. Tamalpais: Man and a Mountain's Resources," *The Californians* 3 (January/February 1985): 36.

138. Memorandum book of Thomas Virgil Hill, the artist's son, in the collection of the Oakland Museum of California, accession number 77.158.6.

139. *San Francisco Chronicle*, 24 August 1879, and *San Francisco News Letter and California Advertiser*, 12 July 1879.

140. *San Francisco Chronicle*, 18 August 1879 and 24 August 1879.

141. *San Francisco Chronicle*, 22 September 1879.

142. This is in keeping with the artist's advice to his son: "Don't paint faces on your figures if a daub of color is enough." Memorandum book of Thomas Virgil Hill, the artist's son, in the collection of the Oakland Museum of California, accession number 77.158.6.

143. *San Francisco Chronicle*, 28 September 1879, and *San Francisco News Letter and California Advertiser*, 4 October 1879.

144. *San Francisco Chronicle*, 10 November 1879.

145. *San Francisco Chronicle*, 17 November 1879 and 8 December 1879.

146. *San Francisco Chronicle*, 3 March 1880.

147. *San Francisco News Letter and California Advertiser*, 3 March 1880.

148. *San Francisco News Letter and California Advertiser*, 13 March 1880.

149. *San Francisco Chronicle*, 9 May 1880, 20 June 1880, and 3 October 1880; *Daily Evening Post* (San Francisco), 1 May 1880; and *Boston Sunday Budget*, 1 August 1880.

150. *San Francisco Examiner*, 28 November 1880.

151. "The Last Spike," *The Californian* 3 (March 1881): 281, and *San Francisco Examiner*, 28 November 1880.

152. *San Francisco Examiner*, 28 November 1880.

153. There is a possibility that Hill hoped *The Driving of the Last Spike* could be used as part of the re-decoration underway at the United States Capitol Building. After much campaigning, Bierstadt was successful in convincing Congress to purchase for the Capitol his *Discovery of the Hudson River* and *Settlement of California, Bay of Monterey, 1770* in 1874 and 1878 respectively. Although *The Driving of the Last Spike* depicted a nationalistic subject, and Hill announced his intention to paint it before the final commission for the Capitol had been decided, he does not appear to have competed for this award. His failure to sell the painting to Stanford or his estate obsessed Hill during his later years. Linda Ferber, "Albert Bierstadt: The History of a Reputation" in Anderson and Ferber, *Albert Bierstadt*, 49–53; Arkelian, *Thomas Hill*, 29; and Thomas Hill, *History of the "Spike Picture," and Why It Is Still in my Possession* (San Francisco: R. R. Hill, n.d.).

154. *Wasp* (San Francisco), 26 March 1881.

155. *San Francisco Chronicle*, 12 July 1881.

156. *San Francisco Examiner*, 27 November 1881.

157. *San Francisco News Letter and California Advertiser*, 4 March 1882.

158. *San Francisco News Letter and California Advertiser*, 4 March 1882.

159. *San Francisco Examiner*, 19 March 1882.

160. *The Argonaut* (San Francisco), 15 July 1882; *San Francisco Daily Evening Post*, 15 August 1882; *San Francisco Examiner*, 20 August 1882; and Hank Johnston, *The Yosemite Grant, 1864–1906: A Pictorial History* (Yosemite National Park, Calif.: Yosemite Association, 1995), 172.

161. *San Francisco Examiner,* 4 February 1883, and *The Argonaut* (San Francisco), 24 February 1883.

162. *San Francisco Chronicle,* 13 January 1884 and 2 February 1884.

163. *San Francisco Chronicle,* 17 August 1884.

164. *San Franciscan,* 1 November 1884.

165. Although Hill traveled through the Rockies several times and recorded a train ride through Colorado in an account he wrote of his 1893 trip to Chicago, there is no evidence he spent any substantial length of time there. Thomas Hill, artist's account book, Crocker Art Museum, accession number 1981.5.44.

166. *San Franciscan,* 29 November 1884.

167. *San Franciscan,* 29 November 1884.

168. *San Franciscan,* 17 January 1885.

169. Report by J. J. Owen from the *San Jose Times-Mercury,* n.d., Richard N. Schellens papers, California Historical Society Library, San Francisco. Also, *San Franciscan,* 28 February 1885 and 28 March 1885. Hill may have been in Boston at this time. See *Boston Evening Transcript,* 16 March 1885.

170. *San Francisco Call,* 28 April 1885.

171. Shirley Sargent, *Yosemite's Historic Wawona* (Yosemite, Calif.: Flying Spur Press, 1979), 41; she refers to Willetta as "Hill's devoted receptionist." Flora Hill McCullough, in memoirs on file at the Yosemite Museum Archives, acknowledges that Hill allowed Estella and Willetta to sell pressed flowers at his Wawona studio as a "concession." Information from Hill's family about this period is sketchy and often contradictory. However, Willetta Hill is consistently noted as a member of Hill's party in press accounts of his travels from the late 1880s.

172. *San Francisco Chronicle,* 9 August 1885.

173. Arkelian, *Thomas Hill,* 32, citing "Declaration of Homestead" by Charlotte M. Hill, 1 March 1887, Alameda County Records, Oakland, California.

174. Hank Johnston, *The Yosemite Grant, 1864–1906: A Pictorial History* (Yosemite National Park, Calif.: Yosemite Association, 1995), 173.

175. *San Francisco News Letter and California Advertiser,* 1 May 1886, and *Daily Evening Post* (San Francisco), 1 May 1886.

176. *White Mountain Echo* (Bethlehem, N.H.), 7 August 1886 and *Sacramento Bee,* 4 September 1886.

177. Minutes of the San Francisco Art Association, 10 December 1886, Archives of American Art, roll 1288. Also, Easton and Eldridge, auctioneers, *Catalogue of Oil Paintings,* 22 December 1886.

178. Easton and Eldridge, *Catalogue of Oil Paintings,* 22 December 1886.

179. Arkelian, *Thomas Hill,* 32; *San Francisco Chronicle,* 23 December 1886; and Minutes of the San Francisco Art Association, 21 December 1886, Archives of American Art, roll 1288.

180. *Daily Evening Post* (San Francisco), 19 March 1887, and Arkelian, *Thomas Hill,* 33.

181. *Daily Evening Post* (San Francisco), 19 March 1887.

182. *San Francisco Call,* 2 September 1894.

183. *San Francisco Examiner,* 29 January 1888.

184. Jay C. Bruce, Sr., *Cougar Killer* (New York: Comet Press Books, 1953), 92.

185. Arkelian, *Thomas Hill,* 34; *Wave,* (San Francisco), 21 January 1893; and *San Francisco Call,* 1 December 1893.

186. *California at the World's Columbian Exposition, Final Report, Chicago, 1893* (Sacramento: State Printing Office, 1894).

187. *San Francisco Call,* 2 September 1894.

188. *San Francisco Call,* 2 September 1894.

189. *San Francisco Call,* 15 December 1894.

190. Elizabeth H. Godfrey, "Thumbnail Sketches of Yosemite Valley—Thomas Hill," *Yosemite Nature Notes* (March 1944): 31.

191.   Jay C. Bruce, Sr., *Cougar Killer*, 84.

192.   *San Francisco Call*, 5 December 1895. A number of references to Princess Louise appear in materials on Hill, including a comment in family records that Hill's daughter Estella Louise, born in 1865, was named after this artistically-inclined member of the British royal family. Estella's birth, however, predated reputed sketching trips Hill and Princess Louise made in 1866 and 1867; furthermore, there is no evidence that Hill visited England during his European sojourn. The *San Francisco Bulletin* of 16 July 1899 stated that "When Princess Louise visited this city, she, who is an enthusiast in art and no mean painter, desired an introduction to Mr. Hill. The meeting was arranged and the princess and painter went together to Monterey, and there made several sketches. The princess was delighted with Mr. Hill and his work. His paintings were familiar to her, and for them she entertained the highest admiration. She commissioned him to paint for her a picture of Yosemite Valley for $2500. He accepted the offer, but when the princess reached England she wrote to Mr. Hill saying she would much prefer him to paint for her a picture of Canadian scenes. She said that the Yosemite Valley was well known in England, while Canada was unknown. A picture representing some of Canada's wild territory would appeal more to Englishmen, and she begged he would paint her a picture. Mr. Hill never went to Canada, and consequently the picture was not painted."

193.   Arkelian, *Thomas Hill*, 37, citing the *San Francisco Chronicle*, 11 January 1896.

194.   For example, the *San Francisco Call* for 23 November 1897 includes an article headlined "HILL HAS RETURNED/Famous Artist Comes to the City/From a Summer Sojourn at His Wawona Studio."

195.   *San Francisco Chronicle*, 8 October 1899.

196.   Thomas Hill, artist's notebook, 1896–1900, Crocker Art Museum, accession number 1981.5.43.

197.   Thomas Hill to John Odiorne (his nephew) 21 May 1900, archives of the Oakland Museum of California.

198.   Thomas Hill to John Odiorne (his nephew) 21 May 1900, archives of the Oakland Museum of California. Documented references to Hill's Southern California sojourns at this time counter beliefs that he was either in Raymond, near Wawona, or at his Yosemite studio during most of the year.

199.   *San Francisco Call*, 9 September 1906.

200.   *The Argonaut* (San Francisco), 12 December 1910.

THE OIL SKETCH IN NINETEENTH-CENTURY AMERICAN PAINTING

WILLIAM H. GERDTS

THE OIL SKETCH HAS NOT ALWAYS enjoyed legitimacy in the American art world. When an anonymous New York critic formulated the hierarchy of pictorial genres in 1827, he was following the precedence and categorization that had been laid down by the French Academy almost two centuries earlier, and which had been repeated, with minor variations, by such artist-theoreticians in Great Britain as Jonathan Richardson, Sir Joshua Reynolds, and Henry Fuseli. His goal was the determination of the relative worth of each category according to the intellectual, emotional, and moral impact of the work of art upon the viewer, and to the relative exercise upon the mind of the artist of each theme—the conviction, in other words, that "mental is superior to manual labor."[1]

It is not our purpose here to debate the author's ten-fold categorization which placed "Epic, Dramatic, and Historic" painting at the most exalted end of the scale, and "Still Life, Dead Game, and Fruit and Flowers" as the least distinguished of themes, among the first eight groupings. But of even *less* esteem, even below the various categories of still life, the writer noted "9. Sketches." and "10. Copies." Copying was noted as a purely mechanical operation. As for sketches, he remarked: "*One* carefully finished object,—if it be but an *apple*,—where attention has been paid to its drawing, its light and shade, and its color, is of more real benefit to the young artist, and more certainly indicative of his talent, than fifty careless, idle scratches."[2]

Though "sketches" was listed among the categories of painting (the author also dealt with sculpture, architecture, and engraving), the critic was referring primarily to pen and ink or pencil sketches, for generally, it would have been considered utter folly in the early nineteenth century for even a presumptuous tyro to pass him- or herself off as a professional artist by exhibiting oil sketches.[3] Our early landscape painters such as Thomas Cole attempted to retain the impress of natural forms in their memories, often with the help of outline drawings and occasional pencil and pen-and-ink sketches of details of trees and rocks, in order to better transmit in the studio the spirit of the landscape to canvas. Pen-and-ink sketches continued to be exhibited from time to time at the National Academy of Design annual shows, but oil sketches were seldom shown until about the middle of the century.

Thomas Hill
(United States, 1829–1908)
Chinese Man Tending Cattle, n.d.
Oil on paper mounted on board, 20½ x 13½ in.
Private collection.

Asher B. Durand appears to have been the first American artist to regularly paint oils out of doors,[4] and was clearly the earliest to *exhibit* landscape sketches. His first, *Landscape. An Autumnal Sketch,* appeared at the academy's 1839 annual exhibition, while a *Study from Nature* was shown at the academy annual in 1844. That the 1839 autumnal landscape was an oil painting is confirmed by the disparaging critic for the *New-Yorker* who complained about Durand's coloration.[5] For the remainder of the 1840s and in the following decade, Durand exhibited landscape studies in oil at the academy annuals and with the American Art-Union in New York.

It was Durand and the French emigré landscapist, Regis Gignoux, who were the most consistent in the display of such pictures before the 1850s; Gignoux exhibited eight "sketches from nature" at the academy in 1843, from among hundreds which he had previously had on display at the Granite Building. These were available for viewing, but it appeared still to have been his intention to transform them into larger and more finished works.[6]

Durand, on the other hand, sold 112 oil studies at auction at Leeds Art Gallery in April of 1867 (and over time gave away and sold a small number of other sketches). In 1864 Matthew Vassar donated two Durand oil studies, *Where the Streamlet Sings in Rural Joy,* ca. 1850, and the 1856 *Through the Woods* (fig. 1), to Vassar College, part of the collection Vassar had acquired from the avid purchaser of American landscapes, Elias Magoon.

As the conceptualized landscapes of the 1820s, '30s, and '40s, composed in the studios and often specifically termed "compositions," gave way to a new respect for the transcriptive landscape, oil studies created directly from nature not only played a more conspicuous role in the formulation of finished pictures but gained aesthetic currency in their own right. Thus, by the 1860s, the artistic merit of the oil study as a true work of art was obviously beginning to be recognized.[7] Durand, for instance, specifically received commissions for oil studies and sketches during the 1850s. One Boston patron, J. C. Gray, wrote: "I understand from Miss Durand that you might perhaps be willing to execute a study for me from nature in the coming summer. I wish for an American landscape. On some accounts I should prefer a sketch directly from nature to a more finished piece." A second letter from Gray indicates that Durand had responded positively on June 19, suggesting a price of $150.[8] Another collector, Robert S. Chilton of Washington, D. C., wrote to Durand that "I am very anxious to have an oil sketch by you—it matters not what, a single tree or a rock."[9]

From the 1840s on, following Durand's lead, landscape painters increasingly treated outdoor oil sketching as an imperative, with those artists particularly close in concept and methodology to Durand (John F. Kensett, especially) engaged in such activity. These mid-century landscapists were intent upon recording the changing effects of sunlight, atmosphere, and the related phenomena of cloud formations and arboreal shadow patterns.

FIGURE 2
Thomas Cole
(United States, 1801–1848)
Study for the Oxbow, 1835–36.
Oil on canvas, 15½ x 20¼ in.
Private collection; photograph courtesy of
Kennedy Galleries, Inc., New York.

Though mountainous regions were novel subjects when American artists such as Thomas Cole first began to record native scenery in the 1820s,[10] (fig. 2) by the middle of the century, summer sketching excursions were the norm for professionals and amateurs alike, made more agreeable by the introduction of an accessible transportation system of highways and railroads, tourist facilities that often catered to artists, and the development of the collapsible metallic tube (for easily transporting oil colors) in 1841 by the American portrait painter, John Goffe Rand. Newspapers and magazines regularly featured articles in June, July, and August, frequently entitled "The Summer Haunts of Our Artists," detailing the rural destinations of American painters, and invariably followed up in September or October with descriptions of the results of the artists' summer sketching, and occasionally with studio visits describing the major works being created on the bases of such sketches and studies.

Complicating any attempt to summarize such efforts was the indiscriminate use of the terms "sketch" and "study." Actually, "studies" appeared in early academy exhibitions a good deal more often than "sketches," the earliest example being a *Study from Nature* submitted by Henry Inman in 1829. This was a figure piece, however, not a landscape, and the frequent uses of the modifier "from nature" with both "sketches" and "studies" did not necessarily indicate landscape subjects; numerous still lifes by George Hall and others were denoted as "from nature," and in such cases, they were certainly finished works and not preparatory for more elaborate compositions. "Sketches" were frequently annotated that they were preliminary to more elaborate works; the earliest such "sketches" shown at the academy were two exhibited in 1832 by Robert Weir called *Composition (Sketch) for a Larger Picture* and *Consecration of a Nun—Sketch for a Larger Picture,* though the latter was not finally realized as a finished work until 1863 as *Taking the Veil* (Yale University Art Gallery, New Haven, Connecticut). Though Durand used the term "sketch" far less frequently than "study," for most artists during the 1830s and '40s they were probably interchangeable.

This was to change, however. Both "landscape studies" and "landscape sketches" appeared with increasing frequency in American exhibitions after the middle of the century, though the designation "study" remained the more common.[11] This was almost certainly due to the prevalence and popularity of the writings of the British aesthetician, John Ruskin, whose artistic theories and beliefs appeared in the earliest significant American art periodical, *The Crayon,* published between 1855 and 1861. Outdoor studies and sketches were the primary and natural products of summer, when the artists abandoned their urban studios to work directly from nature. The first time that such activity was noticed and encouraged by *The Crayon,* one writer—almost surely its artist-editor, William J. Stillman—offered a warning to young painters that: "Beginners should do nothing slightly, but should rather finish a very few things perfectly, than to do any number with half-completeness. A single study made in this spirit will bring more improvement than ten times the amount of labor less earnestly bestowed. And remember that finish does not consist in glossy manipulation, but in the fullness of rendering of the minutiae."[12]

Stillman had already made clear his distinction between the study and the sketch, exulting the former and deprecating the latter, in a review of the annual exhibition of the National Academy. He denounced "the habit of our artists of making broad sketches. . . . The true method of study is, to take small portions of scenes, and there to explore perfectly, and with the most insatiable curiosity, every object presented, and to define them with the carefulness of a topographer. . . . To make a single study of a portion of a landscape in this way, is more worth than a summer's sketching. Young artists should never *sketch,* but always *study,* and especially never make studio sketches."[13]

The group of American followers of Ruskin's dicta, known as the American Pre-Raphaelites, undoubtedly honored the distinction between study and sketch, but most others probably did not. Indeed, the practice of outdoor (especially summer) painting increased, and, despite Ruskinian admonition, artists tended not only to produce more freely sketched studies from nature, but also to exhibit and even offer such works for sale (a practice disdained by the Pre-Raphaelites).[14]

The outdoor studies and sketches of Durand may not have been produced directly with Ruskin's aesthetic principles in mind, but they were nevertheless quite meticulously rendered; in fact, critics held Durand's studies up as models to the artistic community, while decrying the habit of many landscape artists in "making broad sketches without particular reference to detail."[15] But artists of the next generation often exalted in bravura brushwork and expressive freedom of execution, whether painting on their campstools under white umbrellas in the White Mountains, as celebrated in one of Winslow Homer's best-known paintings of the late 1860s, *Artists Sketching in the White Mountains* (fig. 3),[16] or seeking picturesque scenery in Northern France or in the fields and moors of Polling and Dachau in Bavaria.

The popularity of these sketches was expressly acknowledged by the National Academy in 1870 when for its Forty-Fifth Annual Exhibition, the Corridor gallery was given over to a concentration of about 150 oil sketches and studies, including eight by Winslow Homer.[17] Critical reaction was generally disapproving, however, suggesting that the artists should reserve their studies for studio use.[18] It would be over a decade (1882) before the American Art Gallery, a commercial establishment in New York City, would begin to hold a series of exhibitions expressly to celebrate and market artists' sketches.[19]

Homer's examples shown at the academy in 1870 included such genre pieces as his *White Mountain Wagon* (fig. 4), but most of the studies and sketches were landscape and coastal scenes. By 1870, outdoor sketching in oil had become an indispensable activity of all American landscape specialists, and writers and critics increasingly recognized the merits of such outdoor work. Indeed, one commentator in 1876 noted that "with each passing summer a disposition to work more from Nature, and to depend less upon *chic* in the finish of pictures. . . . many a sketch has become an embroidered lie by undergoing the 'final touches' of the studio. Keep to Nature, good friends of the palette and brush! . . . The best work that comes yearly to the studios is sure to be the first frank sketches made out of doors, and never retouched. If done for the love of doing, it has something of the savor of inspiration, however crudely left."[20]

The two artists whose oil sketches have earned most celebrity among scholars and collectors today are Frederic Edwin Church and Albert Bierstadt. Church, the most renowned of Thomas Cole's few students, was surely aware of Cole's involvement with sketching in oil, as well as that of Cole's good friend and colleague, Durand. But Church practiced oil sketching to a far greater degree than either; with almost seven hundred oil sketches and studies remaining in his studio on his death in 1900, he was probably the most prolific American practitioner of the century.[21]

Only a relatively few oil sketches, such as his *Mount Chimborazo, Ecuador* (fig. 5), have survived from Church's two trips to western South America in 1853 and 1857, journeys inspired in part by Alexander von Humboldt's *Kosmos,* first published in 1845, and translated into English as *Cosmos* in 1849. Von Humboldt opined that "Colored sketches, taken directly from nature, are the only means by which an artist, on his return, may reproduce the character of distant regions in more elaborately finished pictures; and this object will be the more fully attained where the painter has, at the same time, drawn or painted directly from nature a large number of separate studies of the foliage of trees; of leafy, flowering or fruit-bearing stems; of prostrate trunks, overgrown with Pothos and Orchideae; of rocks and of portions of the shore, and the soil of the forest. The possession of such correctly drawn and well proportioned sketches will enable the artist to dispense with all the deceptive aid of hothouse forms, and so-called botanical

FIGURE 3
Winslow Homer
(United States, 1836–1910)
Artists Sketching in the White Mountains, 1868.
Oil on panel, 9½ x 15⅞ in.
Portland Museum of Art, Maine;
bequest of Charles Shipman Payson.

FIGURE 4
Winslow Homer
White Mountain Wagon, 1856.
Oil on canvas, 15½ x 20¼ in.
Cooper Hewitt National Academy of Design
Museum, Smithsonian Institution, New York.

delineations."[22] This provided a clear formula not only for the construct of Church's much-acclaimed paintings of South America, but for his vast panoramic landscapes of North America, the island of Jamaica, the Arctic regions, Europe, and the Near East. Church's oil sketches, however, done on cardboard, occasionally canvas or paper, and most often on thin cream-colored board, were almost never transferred directly to the larger canvases, but rather offered extracted details that were combined in the final work.[23]

In his later years, when in semi-retirement and ensconced in his palatial home, "Olana," near Hudson, New York, Church indulged in oil studies of clouds, light, and atmosphere executed with extraordinary breadth, experiments in paint for their own sake and usually divorced from considerations for finished pictures.[24] Unlike Durand, however, Church appears neither to have exhibited nor sold his sketches, though one is inscribed on the reverse with "South America $300/by Fr. E. Church." While art writers not infrequently commented on Church's studies during visits to his studio, the oil sketches otherwise remained pictorial aids in the manufacture of his completed landscapes as Von Humboldt had counseled.[25]

The best-known oil sketches by Albert Bierstadt are those painted on his numerous voyages to the American West, but Bierstadt had begun to create such studies during his years studying in Düsseldorf, Germany, from 1853 to 1856.[26] His colleague and studio-mate there, Worthington Whittredge, related that in 1855 Bierstadt borrowed "a paint box, stool and umbrella which he put with a few pieces of clothing into a large knapsack, and shouldering it one cold April morning he started off to try his luck among the Westphalian peasants where he expected to work. He remained away without a word to us until late autumn when he returned loaded down with innumerable studies of all sorts, oaks, roadsides, meadows, glimpses of water, exteriors of Westphalian cottages, and one very remarkable study of sunlight on the steps of an old church (fig. 6) which some years afterwards was turned into a picture that gave him more fame than anything he had ever painted. . . . He set to work in my studio immediately on large canvases composing and putting together parts of studies he had made, and worked with an industry which left no daylight to go to waste."[27]

Two years after his return to America in 1857, Bierstadt made his first trip west, inspired by the growing fascination with reports of this distant region following the gold rush of 1848 and the growth of settlements that ensued, and probably spurred on by the fame and success achieved by Frederic Church with his previously unfamiliar scenes of exotic South American landscapes. Once in the West, first in the Rockies in 1859, and then on to California on his subsequent trips beginning in 1863, Bierstadt created hundreds of oil sketches on paper, composition board, cardboard, panel, and canvas. These he classified and inserted into wooden screens in his studios back east for use in the creation of his panoramic Western canvases.

In a letter written while in the Rocky Mountains to *The Crayon* during his first trip west, Bierstadt reported not only on his sketches of Western scenery, but also on the Native Americans: "When I am making studies in color, the Indians seem much pleased to look on and see me work; they have an idea that I am some strange medicine-man."[28] Bierstadt's sketches range from studies that were recognized as almost completed paintings in small format, to those that are near abstract arrangements of form and color. The

FIGURE 6
Albert Bierstadt
(United States, 1830–1902)
Sunlight and Shadow, 1855.
Oil on paper, 18½ x 13 in.
The Newark Museum, New Jersey; gift of
Dr. J. Ackerman Coles.

FIGURE 7
Albert Bierstadt
Yosemite Valley, California, 1863.
Oil on paper mounted on canvas, 16 x 20 in.
Lowe Art Museum, Coral Gables, Florida.

former were tremendously commented upon and admired in Bierstadt's life-time, especially those painted in California, such as *Yosemite Valley, California* (fig. 7). Charles H. Webb, on seeing the oil sketches Bierstadt brought back from his first visit to Yosemite, wrote: "For his sketch of 'The Dome,' I would give more than I would for any finished picture that San Francisco contains. Sketch, did I say—they are not sketches, nor are they studies—they are pictures, and need but frames and the faintest re-touch to entitle them to a place in any gallery."[29] The latter group of more generalized landscape studies was among those that first attracted modern attention, revealing certain affinities with contemporary art of the 1950s and '60s, and has been the subject of a number of more recent exhibitions.[30]

An especially detailed report of Bierstadt's store of sketches appeared in a Utica, New York, newspaper in 1874, when the artist was working in Water-ville on his *Discovery of the Hudson River,* which he sold to Congress the following year:

> These sketches, let me observe, are mostly in oil, upon loose sheets of canvas, and were made in the open air in all seasons of the year, not excepting winter. They are classified, for the most part, according to the county or district where they were made, and are arranged in separate portfolios kept in closets or trunks, so that any sketch which may be wanted for a particular purpose can be found without a moment's delay. The California sketches were most numerous. here were groups and single specimens of the famous *Sequoia gigantea* and of many other trees of that wonderful country. here were the snowy Sierras and the waterfalls and strange mountain-forms of the Yosemite valley. As the contents of these portfolios were slowly turned over it required no laborious searching to discover the original materials of several of our artist's great California pictures. Other port-

folios contained sketches made in different countries of Europe and in Oregon, and among the White Hills of New Hampshire, and in several portions of the eastern States. Aside from these were there miscellaneous studies—effects caught at the moment—of sunrises and sunsets, of clear skies and cloudy skies, of mists and rainbows, of thunder-storms, of wild-tossed forests and grain fields, and the clear shining of the sun after rain. Surely, no one on looking at these sketches, could doubt that this artist is a sincere lover of nature.[31]

Unlike Church, Bierstadt appears to have exhibited and sold his oil studies from time to time; in 1865, "sketches" by Bierstadt, owned by E. Jenkins, were exhibited at the newly established California Art Union in San Francisco. And perhaps during his later years, when his vast canvases fell out of fashion, commissions were no longer plentiful, and the "sketch aesthetic" had achieved a popularity of its own, he disposed of more.

While it is probable that all professional artists of this generation painted numerous oil studies, it may be that painters such as Church, Bierstadt, and Thomas Hill relied especially upon such work. Because they visited very exotic and sometimes spectacular scenery that was not easily accessible, some of their subjects would have been difficult or even impossible to confirm on return expeditions. For the generation of artists that followed Church, Bierstadt, and Hill, then, the finished painting, particularly in landscape, often became indistinguishable from the sketch, especially when impressionism became the aesthetic of choice. But the same goals and meanings that the impressionists sought had motivated those earlier artists. As one impassioned proponent of the sketch noted in 1896: "Reproduce faithfully tree, stream and mountain, and what have you done? Shown, perhaps, some study, some technical skill. But, if you catch the pathos that steals over the meadows with the evening mist, or the joy singing in the blaze of Spring sunshine, you have entered the realm of poetry, left the rank of those who 'having eyes see not,' and joined the company of the select who can find 'every common bush ablaze with God.'. . . The path does not end where it disappears behind that clump of trees; the sea is sweeping away for league upon league beyond the apparent horizon. So the sketch of the mountain, if a true impression and not a mere reproduction, should suggest the grandeur of all mountains, the sketch of the plain the beauty of all plains."[32] And so do the sketches of Albert Bierstadt, Frederic Church, and Thomas Hill sweep beyond the apparent horizon, and suggest the grandeur of all mountains.

I have benefitted greatly here from an unpublished study by Elizabeth Wylie, "Plein-Air Painting in Nineteenth-Century America," prepared at the Graduate School of the City University of New York in February, 1987, as a Qualifying Paper for the Institute of Fine Arts, New York University.

1.   "Review. The Exhibition of the National Academy of Design, 1827. The Second. New York. D. Fanshaw. 1827," *United States Review and Literary Gazette,* 2 (July 1827): 241–263. This article previously has been referenced as authored by Fanshaw by a number of scholars, including myself. In actuality, Daniel Fanshaw was a New York printer; he also printed the National Academy's first constitution. While it is conceivable that he may have written this review, there is really no compelling reason to attribute it to him. His name is mentioned in the title here because the "Review," though it *does* provide an exhaustive critique of the academy's second annual exhibition, is nominally an examination, not of the show, but of the catalogue.

In a more diffused fashion, the hierarchy of genres had actually been discussed a generation earlier in the United States in a three-part article that appeared in the *Christian's, Scholar's and Farmer's Magazine,* December–January 1789–90, 595–598; February–March 1790, 719–722; and April–May 1790, 80–83. In the third part on page 83, the "Sketch" and "Studies" were discussed and differentiated, though not evaluated. The former was defined as "the first tracing of a picture, or the first idea of a design.—There are two sorts of sketches, the one is with chalk, and the other with colours; the latter is an essay of a larger work which the painter meditates." Studies were defined as "different designs of figures, or essays which painters make of parts of some great work."

2.   "Review," *United States Review and Literary Gazette,* 258.

3.   "Review," *United States Review and Literary Gazette,* 258. The writer referred specifically to George W. Hatch, soon to become one of the more important engravers of his generation, who first appeared in the academy annual in 1827, exhibiting a group of sketches, along with another single work, *Sketch, Beggar's Petition.* Hatch was a stu-

dent in the academy's first class, which began in January, 1826. The one significant exception to the absence of the display of landscape sketches in oil was the exhibition of eight oil sketches (five specifically designated as landscapes) by Charles Willson Peale at the Sixth Annual Exhibition of the Pennsylvania Academy of the Fine Arts. But though publicly exhibited, these landscapes, all created in the vicinity of Belfield, his country home, were painted by Peale in his old age for amusement rather than to achieve professional distinction. Ultimately he completed fourteen of these small pictures, which were put on display at his museum in Philadelphia in 1822. See Jessie Poesch, "Germantown Landscapes: A Peale Family Amusement," *Antiques* 72 (November 1957): 434–39, and Charles Coleman Sellers, "Charles Willson Peale with Patron and Populace," *Transactions of the American Philosophical Society,* part 3, 59 (1969): 41–2.

4.   Daniel Huntington, *Asher B. Durand; Memorial Address* (New York: Century Association, 1887), 28. He noted that Durand was "a pioneer in another very important branch of study, viz., that of painting carefully finished studies directly from nature out-of-doors." Huntington's portrait of Durand (1857, Century Association, New York City) depicts Durand seated in a landscape with an oil study for *Franconia Notch* on his easel; Durand himself painted this study within Huntington's portrait. Durand's finished composition, also titled *White Mountain Scenery, Franconia Notch, N. H.,* on extended loan to The New-York Historical Society, is owned by the New York Public Library.

5.   "Exhibition of the National Academy of Design," *The New-Yorker* 8 (11 May 1839): 125.

6.   "The World of Art," *New World* 6 (25 March 1843): 368.

7.   David B. Lawall, "Asher B. Durand: His Art and Art Theory in Relation to His Times" (Ph.D. diss., Princeton University, 1966), vol. 3, 211–268; and David B. Lawall, *Asher B. Durand: A Documentary Catalogue of the Narrative and Landscape Paintings* (New York & London: Garland Publishing, Inc., 1978), 169–208.

8.   J. C. Gray to Durand, 11 June 1854 and 22 June 1854, collection of the New York Public Library.

9.   Robert. S. Chilton to Durand, 5 March 1857, collection of the New York Public Library. Both this and the Gray letter are cited by Barbara Novak in *American Painting of the 19th Century: Realism, Idealism and the American Experience* (New York: Praeger Publishers, 1969), 87–8. In this section of her classic tome, Dr. Novak is especially perceptive about Durand's sketches from nature.

10.   Outdoor oil sketches by Cole are known, especially beginning with his first trip to Italy in 1831–32, but they do not seem to have figured in the development of his final studio productions to anywhere near the extent that they were depended on by later generations of American landscape artists. Many of his oil sketches would themselves appear to be studio productions. The largest group of Cole's oil studies are reproduced in Kennedy Galleries, Inc., *An Exhibition of Paintings by Thomas Cole N. A. from the Artist's Studio, Catskill, New York* (New York: Kennedy Galleries, Inc., 1964). In October of 1843, William Sidney Mount was visiting Cole at his home in Catskill, New York, where both painted in oils out-of-doors, and from then on Mount was painting outdoors with great regularity. Alfred Frankenstein, *William Sidney Mount* (New York: Harry N. Abrams, Inc., 1975), 66.

11.   Though this analysis has concentrated especially on the annual exhibitions of the National Academy of Design in New York City, landscape sketches and studies, the latter almost always designated "from nature," began to appear in the annual shows of the Boston Athenaeum only in the 1850s. Excepting the eight oil sketches shown by Charles Willson Peale in 1818, the only such works to appear in the annuals held at the Pennsylvania Academy of the Fine Arts in Philadelphia were a group of studies and sketches on the Juniata River shown by Russell Smith in the late 1830s and early '40s.

At the academy, even during the 1850s and '60s, studies and sketches were fairly infrequently displayed, aside from an unusual group of almost a dozen oil sketches of Venice exhibited in 1858 by Enoch Wood Perry, who had been the American consul there for over a year. There were only singular exceptions by artists such as Asher B. Durand, Regis Gignoux, William Hart, and others mentioned elsewhere in this essay, and an occasional work by painters (such as John Henry Hill, Aaron Shattuck, and William Trost Richards) associated with John Ruskin's aesthetic theories.

The little-known and short-lived James Harrison Lambdin, son of the portraitist, James Reid Lambdin, and younger brother of the still-life and genre painter, George Cochran Lambdin, showed *only* sketches and studies during the brief period from 1859–62 that he exhibited works at the academy; it is likely that these also adhered to Ruskin-inspired strategies. Enlisting in August, 1862, the younger Lambdin was wounded in the Civil War, and abandoned his artistic career after he left the service in 1865. See Ruth Irwin Weidner, *George Cochran Lambdin 1830–1896* (Chadds Ford, Penn.: Brandywine River Museum, 1986), 18.

12.   [William J. Stillman?], "Studying from Nature," *The Crayon* 1 (6 June 1855): 353.

13.   [William J. Stillman?], "The Academy Exhibition.—No. 1," *The Crayon* 1 (28 March 1855): 203. See also [Stillman?], "Studying from Nature," 353–354. This Ruskinian distinction between "sketch" and "study" had been made earlier, though in regard to drawing rather than painting; this was published in 1847, the same year that Ruskin's writings first appeared in an American edition. See John Gadsby Chapman, *The American Drawing Book* (New York: J. S. Redfield, 1847), 168–9: "A Study and a Sketch are too commonly considered identical in meaning. A *Sketch* is but a graphic memorandum—an expedient; a *Study*, the more faithful record of a well-digested investigation. However well a sketch may serve to retain a transitory impression, and, to some extent, give it intelligible expression, its practical value and service rests in the service of higher capacity, only attainable by severer study. . . . The value of careful study, and drawing from nature, consists not so much in the production of an elaborate work, as in the familiarity thereby obtained with the object of imitation."

14. In an article that appeared in July, 1864 in *The New Path,* the official periodical forum for the American Pre-Raphaelites, a writer stated that: "It is not well for young students of art to try and sell their studies, because they will constantly be tempted by the desire to make them popular and pleasing. We do not forbid the lover of true art to buy a good study . . . but the would-be connoisseur is considered a detected jack-daw if he call anything a picture but a somewhat elaborate oil painting." "Pictures and Studies," *The New Path* 2 (July 1864): 37.

15. [Stillman?], "The Academy Exhibition,—No. 1," 203.

16. For a typical reaction at this time to the increased popularity of outdoor sketching, in an article whose title calls to mind Homer's 1868 picture, see Edmund Clark, "Under the Sketching Umbrella," *Art Review* 1 (August 1871): 4–5.

17. The critic for *The Nation* noted that all the "studies" in the densely-hung corridor were in oil colors and that there were no drawings or other ephemeral media. "Fine Arts. Forty-Fifth Exhibition of the National Academy of Design," *The Nation* 10 (28 April 1870): 278.

18. At least one critic reacted negatively to this profusion of sketches: "The Corridor is crowded with sketches that profess to be nothing more; masses, we may say of them, covering a great many square feet of wall. Winslow Homer, and J. O. Eaton, and Wm. Hart, and Kruseman Van Elten, have brought out from their limbo of studies, it would seem, of years, and spread them out on the walls, for what purpose it is difficult to conjecture; not surely in the hope that they will be purchased; certainly not in the belief that they will be admired. The principal thoughts they suggest is that the finished work is not so much better than the sketches as it ought to be." "Fine Arts. The Landscapes at the Academy," *New York Daily Tribune,* 30 April 1870, 5.

19. The first of these shows was held in the summer of 1882, mounted by the Society of American Artists on the premises of the American Art Gallery, which had begun operation in 1879. By the end of that year, the American Art Gallery was liquidated, but it was soon reconstituted as the American Art Association. It opened on January 1, 1883, and that October held "The Second Annual Exhibition of Sketches and Studies," a show of almost four hundred oil and watercolor sketches by American artists. A third annual exhibition of "Artists' Sketches and Studies" was held in December of 1884. See Gerald D. Bolas, "The American Art Association in the Nineteenth Century," (paper for the City University of New York Graduate School, 1987), 14–27. Bolas is presently completing a dissertation on the American Art Association.

In the autumn of 1891, The Fellowcraft Club in New York City held an "Exhibition of Artists Scraps & Sketches." See William Lewis Fraser, "Exhibition of Artists Scraps & Sketches," *Century Magazine* 42 (October 1891): 96–103. Curiously, as far back as 1813, an unidentified individual in Philadelphia proposed the inauguration of annual exhibitions and sales of artists' studies! See "A Friend to the Arts" and "To the Artists of the City of Philadelphia," *United States Gazette* 44 (6 December 1813): 3. In contrast to this exceptional recommendation, it was almost a century later, in 1912, that the architect and art critic, Russell Sturgis, advocated the founding of a Museum of Studies. See Russell Sturgis, "As to a Museum of Studies," *Scribner's Magazine* 42 (December 1912): 765–8.

20. "Art Matters," *American Art Journal* 26 (7 October 1876): 7.

21. The standard studies of Church's oil sketches are Theodore Stebbins, *Close Observation: Selected Oil Sketches by Frederic Edwin Church* (Washington, D. C.: Smithsonian Institution Press, 1978), and, more recently, Elaine Evans Dee, *Frederic E. Church: Under Changing Skies* (Philadelphia: University of Pennsylvania, 1992). See also David Steadman, "Oil Sketches by Frederic E. Church," *American Art Review* 3 (January–February 1976): 116–122.

22. Alexander Von Humboldt, *Cosmos: A Sketch of a Physical Description of the Universe,* vol. 2 (London: Henry G. Bohn, 1849), 452–3.

23. A rare exception here is Church's Sketch for *Sunrise off the Maine Coast* (Cooper Hewitt National Academy of Design Museum, Smithsonian Institution, New York City), that is almost identical to the more detailed large oil painting, *Sunrise off the Maine Coast* (1863, Wadsworth Atheneum,

Hartford, Connecticut). See Theodore Stebbins, *Close Observation: Selected Oil Sketches by Frederic Edwin Church* (Washington, D.C.: Smithsonian Institution Press, 1978), 21.

24.   Stebbins discusses these late oil sketches at length and with much eloquence, comparing them to John Constable's sky studies of half a century earlier. See Stebbins, *Close Observation*, 45–6.

25.   See Elaine Evans Dee, *Frederic E. Church: Under Changing Skies* (Philadelphia: University of Pennsylvania, 1992), 41–44.

26.   There are two unpublished master's theses on Bierstadt's oil sketches: Claudia Joan Himmelberg, "The Oil Sketches of Albert Bierstadt," University of California, Santa Barbara, 1978, and Carolyn Mae Appleton, "Albert Bierstadt's Early Oil Sketches: 1854–1859," University of Texas at Austin, 1985.

27.   John I. H. Baur, ed., "The Autobiography of Worthington Whittredge, 1820–1910," *Brooklyn Museum Journal* 1 (1942): 26–27. Bierstadt enlarged his study of a church exterior into *Sunlight and Shadow* in 1862 (Fine Arts Museums of San Francisco).

28.   Letter from Bierstadt, 10 July 1859, in "Country Comments," *The Crayon* 6 (September 1859): 287.

29.   Inigo [Charles H. Webb], "Bierstadt's Sketches," *The Golden Era,* 27 September 1863, 5. I am grateful to my good friend, the great scholar of early California art, Alfred Harrison, for this material and the author's identification. Another writer observed that: "Some of his smallest oil sketches in Yosemite give a better idea of its vast dimensions than even the superb photographs of Watkins, or the most carefully finished paintings of other artists." See Benjamin E. Avery, "Art Beginnings in the Pacific II," *Overland Monthly* 1 (August 1868): 114. A third critic noted: "Mr. Bierstadt is one of the most industrious of the votaries of Art. Wherever he may be, he is always at work. His sketches and studies in oil, many of which would pass for finished pictures, are numbered by hundreds." "Albert Bierstadt," *California Art Gallery* 1 (April 1873): 50.

30.   See Florence Lewison, "The Uniqueness of Albert Bierstadt," *American Artist* 28 (September 1964): 28–33, 72, 74. Ms. Lewison mounted three exhibitions of Bierstadt's sketches at her New York gallery: *The Creative Core of Bierstadt—The Abstract Basis of His Art*, 1963; *Man, Beast and Nature,* 1964; and *Bierstadt: His Small Paintings,* 1968. In addition, see Davis & Langdale Company, *Oil Sketches by Albert Bierstadt 1830–1902* (New York, 1982), and Fred A. Myers, "Bierstadt's Small Paintings: The Intimate Aspects of Grand Opera," *Gilcrease Magazine of American History and Art* 7 (September 1985): 1–9.

31.   "Bierstadt in His Studio," *Utica Morning Herald,* 16 September 1874.

32.   N. E. Greenlaw, "Impressionism in Sketching," *Art Interchange* 37 (July 1896): 7.

THOMAS HILL CHRONOLOGY

1829	Born, Birmingham, England, around September 11.
1844	With family, joins father in United States and is employed in a cotton factory.
1845	Works for a carriage painter.
1847	Hired by an interior decoration firm in Boston.
1848–58	Meets Virgil Williams in Boston or White Mountains.
1851	Son Edward Rufus born. Marries Charlotte Elizabeth Hawkes, in Boston.
NO DATE	Twins, Thomas, Jr. and Agnes, die in infancy of diphtheria.
1853	Moves to Philadelphia; attends Pennsylvania School of Fine Arts. Awarded a silver medal for a fruit and flower study at Maryland Institute.
1854	Begins painting in White Mountains.
1855	Moves to Cambridge, Massachusetts.
1856	Listed in *Boston Business Directory,* with studio at Assembly Hall, home in Chelsea.
1858	Son Robert Rembrandt Hill born. Exhibits thirty oil paintings at Leonard and Company in Boston.
1859	Daughter Charlotte born.
1859–60	Employed by Levi-Heywood as a furniture decorator.
1860	Daughter Adeline born in Gardner, Massachusetts.
1861	Listed in *Boston Business Directory,* with home at 4 Irving Street.
APRIL	Departs for California.
1862	Listed in 1862–63 *Langley's San Francisco Directory* as portrait painter, at 420 Montgomery Street.

1860–65		Daughter Ellen Elizabeth (Nellie) born.
1863	JULY	Exhibits paintings at Jones, Wooll and Sutherland, art suppliers.
1864	AUGUST	Contributes a Sierra Nevada lake scene to Grand Fair of the Ladies Christian Commission, to benefit suffering Civil War heroes.
	OCTOBER	Exhibits six landscapes, six portraits, and a "fancy" sketch at Mechanics' Institute and Library, Industrial Exhibition. His paintings displayed in same gallery as photographs by Carleton Watkins.
1865		Daughter Estella Louise born.
	JANUARY	Exhibits two views of Napa Valley, some oil portraits, and a scene of a damsel in sunlight titled *Good Morning* at opening of Art Union.
	APRIL	Sales to San Francisco residents from Art Union gallery include a view of Crystal Springs in San Mateo Co.
	AUGUST	Visits Yosemite with Virgil Williams and Carleton Watkins.
	OCTOBER	Three Yosemite scenes on exhibit at Art Union.
	NOVEMBER	Exhibits painting of Mount Hood.
	DECEMBER	Sells large painting of Yosemite Valley to a Californian for $800.
1866	SUMMER	Leaves California for New York, then France.
1867	MAY	Returns to United States. Opens studio in Boston (No. 48 Studio Building).
1868		Listed in *Boston Business Directory,* 49 Studio Building and home at Cambridge. Designs front cover and frontispiece for *Was It a Ghost? The Murders in Bussey's Wood. An Extraordinary Narrative.*
	JUNE	Exhibits monumental *Yosemite Valley* at Childs Gallery, Boston.
	OCTOBER	With Charles Brainard, visits Whittier's birthplace in East Haverhill.
	NOVEMBER	Noted as working on a picture of Goodrich Falls, and having orders for large pictures of White Mountain scenery. Painting of Whittier home to be chromolithographed by Prang. Displays sketches of Niagara, White Mountain views, and a Chocurua Mountain at Studio Building. Exhibits a mountain lake scene at Jones & Wooll in San Francisco.
1869		Exhibits two paintings, *On the Yuba River* and *Table Mountain, California,* at Snow and Roos, in San Francisco.

Large *Yosemite Valley,* now in collection of Charles Crocker, exhibited at Snow and Roos to high acclaim. Makes studies in White Mountains.

1870		Daughter Laura Bell Hill born.
	FEBRUARY	Sends four paintings from Boston, largest of which is a view of Niagara Falls from the American side, for exhibition and sale in San Francisco.
	DECEMBER	Exhibits large painting of *White Mountain Notch,* a view of Wayside Inn, and eastern Pennsylvania scenes at Childs & Co. in Boston.
1871	JANUARY	Exhibits *Yosemite Valley* at Boston Atheneum. At work in new studio in Cambridge.
	NOVEMBER	Attends meeting of the San Francisco Art Association. Exhibits *Great Cañon of the Sierra, Yosemite* at Room 22, Studio Building, Boston.
	DECEMBER	Exhibits two studies, a wood interior with man fishing and a Yosemite view, at Art Club in Boston.
1872		Son Thomas Virgil Troyon Hill born.
	JANUARY	*Great Cañon of the Sierra, Yosemite* on view at Palette Club in New York.
	LATE SPRING	Guest of Virgil Williams in Sonoma, near San Francisco. Participates in Second Exhibition of San Francisco Art Association.
	MAY	Exhibits *View of South Dome, Yosemite Valley, California* in Boston. Exhibits *Great Cañon of the Sierra, Yosemite* at Snow and Roos in San Francisco, on loan from E. B. Crocker.
	JUNE	Exhibits *Reminiscence of Emerald Bay* at Snow and Roos. Exhibits *Colorado* at San Francisco Art Association.
	AUGUST	Visits Massachusetts; returns to California with his family the following month.
	NOVEMBER	Opens a studio in Tucker's building, San Francisco.
	DECEMBER	Exhibits oil sketches at San Francisco Art Association.
1873		Member of Boston Art Club. Exhibits *Artist's Brook* at Boston Atheneum.
	JANUARY	Exhibits *The Royal Arches of Yosemite* at Gallery of the Art Association.
	FEBRUARY	Joins Bohemian Club.
	MARCH	Exhibits an oil study, *Mount Washington,* at the Boston Art Club.
	APRIL	Exhibits two Sonoma Valley scenes at Snow and Roos in San Francisco. Appointed to Reception Committee of San Francisco Art Association.

	MAY–JUNE	Offers *Lake Tahoe, California, The Great Oak in the Forest at Fontainebleau,* and two wood scenes from nature at Blakeslee and Noyes, Boston.
	MAY	Exhibits *A Forest Scene, Morning in Knight's Valley, Russian River Valley,* and *Connecticut River* at San Francisco Art Association.
	JUNE	Participates in artists' sale at San Francisco Art Association.
	AUGUST	Sketches with William Marple at Donner Lake and travels on to Yosemite.
	OCTOBER	Works on commission for Yosemite paintings for William Ralston and on painting entitled *Donner Lake.* *Home of the Eagle* photographed by Carleton Watkins.
	NOVEMBER	Moves into his new studio in Duncan's Building, on California Street. Appointed to Committee on School of Design of San Francisco Art Association.
	DECEMBER	Nominates Virgil Williams as director of School of Design.
1874		Exhibits large *Source of the Saco* and four oil sketches of Mount St. Helena area.
	MARCH	Exhibits views of Cascade Lake and Emerald Bay at San Francisco Art Association. Appointed member of Committee on School of Design; elected First Vice President of School of Design.
	APRIL	Conducts an auction sale of eighty-three works, mostly oil sketches.
	JULY	Sketching in Utah.
	SEPTEMBER	Announces intention to paint *The Driving of the Last Spike.*
	OCTOBER	In poor health; recuperates in San Mateo.
	NOVEMBER	Is cited as operating his own art gallery on Post Street.
1875	JANUARY	Contributes paintings of Lake Geneva and Falls of Staubach in Switzerland to San Francisco Art Association exhibition. Finishes large oil, *In the Heart of the Sierra,* on commission from E. J. Baldwin, which is exhibited at the San Francisco Art Association to great acclaim.
	JUNE	Exhibits small paintings, *Gathering Flowers (Butterflies)* and *Trout Fishing,* at Art Association. Visits Boston, where exhibits work at Williams and Everett's. Travels to White Mountains and also purchases "Eastern work" for sale at Joseph Roos & Co.
	JULY	Returns to San Francisco.
	NOVEMBER	Finishes large painting, *Donner Lake,* for Collis Huntington.
	DECEMBER	Exhibits two small landscape studies of the White Mountains at Joseph Roos's Gallery in San Francisco.

1876	JANUARY	Exhibits paintings, *Donner Lake* and *Yosemite Valley*, at the San Francisco Art Association.
		Exhibits *Wood Interior* at Boston Art Club.
	MAY	Acquires Beaux Arts Gallery from Joseph Roos.
	JULY	Exhibits White Mountain landscapes at his gallery.
		Departs San Francisco for a sketching trip in the country.
	AUGUST	Exhibits studies made in New Hampshire at Roos & Co.
	SEPTEMBER	Departs for Philadelphia Centennial, where received gold medal for *Donner Lake, Yosemite Valley,* and *Home of the Eagle.*
1877	JANUARY	Completes large painting entitled *Purissima Falls.*
	APRIL	Places ninety-eight paintings, including "many sketches," for an auction held at the San Francisco Art Association.
	JUNE	Travels to St. Helena, Mendocino County.
		Takes an extended sketching trip to Mount Shasta.
	AUGUST	Eleven large paintings by Hill, mostly Yosemite subjects, destroyed by fire in Lick House in San Francisco. Hill, Denny, and Marple receive commissions for replacement paintings for this hotel.
	SEPTEMBER	Exhibits *Yosemite Falls* and *Mount Shasta from Sisson's* for Lick House and *Lake Ralphine* at the San Francisco Art Association.
	DECEMBER	Works on *The Driving of the Last Spike.*
1878		Member, Boston Art Club.
		Biographical sketch appears in *Pacific Coast Mining Review.*
	SPRING	At work on *The Driving of the Last Spike.*
	JUNE	Exhibits painting of New England wood scene at Morris, Schwab & Co., San Francisco.
	JULY	Travels to Oregon and Washington Territory, returning in late August.
	AUGUST	Daughter Flora Camille Frances Hill born.
1879	MARCH	Exhibits canvas entitled *California.*
		Moves into new studio on Turk Street in San Francisco.
		Sells art gallery to Snow and Company.
		Charlotte Hill purchases large home and lot in Oakland.
	JUNE	Travels to Yosemite on a sketching tour, staying for nearly two months.
	OCTOBER	Works on paintings made from sketches made in Yosemite.
	NOVEMBER	Stops working on Yosemite subjects; returns to sketches made in Oregon the previous year.
		Takes leave of studio in San Francisco's Nevada Block to paint at Oakland residence.
1880	MARCH	Exhibits *The Salmon Festival* at the San Francisco Art Association.

	APRIL	Works on *The Driving of the Last Spike* at his home.
	JUNE	Visits Boston and New Hampshire; returns to San Francisco in October.
1881		Member, Boston Art Club.
	JANUARY	Exhibits *The Driving of the Last Spike* at the San Francisco Art Association.
	MARCH	Exhibits oil sketches at San Francisco Art Association.
	JUNE	In Yosemite.
	JULY	Resident at Profile House, a well-known hotel in the White Mountains.
1882	MARCH	Places 120 paintings and oil sketches up for auction in San Francisco.
	MAY	Travels to Yosemite, returning to San Francisco in August.
	NOVEMBER	Occupies new studio in the Mechanics' Library Building in San Francisco.
1883		Member, Boston Art Club.
	SUMMER	Sketches at Yosemite.
1884	MAY	Exhibits large Yosemite painting at San Francisco Art Association.
	JUNE	Works at studio at Clark's, in the Big Trees, near Wawona.
	AUGUST	Returns from Yosemite; departs for Yellowstone.
	NOVEMBER	Returns from Yellowstone and proceeds to studio at Clark's Station. Exhibits *Grand Canyon of the Yellowstone.*
1885	JANUARY	To New Orleans, where exhibits *Grand Canyon of the Yellowstone, Yosemite Valley,* and *The Driving of the Last Spike* at World's Industrial and Cotton Exposition.
	MARCH	Returns from New Orleans.
	APRIL	Daughter Estella Hill marries John Washburn.
	SPRING AND SUMMER	In Yosemite.
1886	APRIL	Exhibits paintings, *Headwater of the Madison River* and *Yellowstone Lake,* as well as Yosemite works at San Francisco Art Association.
	JULY	Father and mother die in Massachusetts. Washburns construct a studio for Hill at Wawona.
	AUGUST	Stays at the Kearsarge House in North Conway, New Hampshire.
	SEPTEMBER	Exhibits *Grand Canyon of the Yellowstone* at California State Fair.
	DECEMBER	Virgil Williams dies. Volunteers to serve as interim director of School of Design without compensation. Holds auction sale of 200 paintings.

1887	MARCH	Leaves post at Art Association to travel to Alaska.
	SEPTEMBER	Exhibits *Yellowstone Canyon* and *Yosemite* at Mechanics' Institute.
1888		Designs embossed covers for and contributes sketches to *In the Heart of the Sierras—The Yosemite Valley* (Oakland: Pacific Coast Publishing House).
	AUGUST	Displays *Mount Tacoma, Royal Arches and Dome, Yosemite,* and *Bass Fishing (Lake George)* at Mechanics' Institute Exhibition.
1889	APRIL	Exhibits *Muir Glacier* and scenes of Yosemite and Lake George.
1891	MAY	Exhibits *The Grand Canyon of the Colorado from near Flagstaff, Arizona* and *Sir Donald Peak in the Selkirk Mountains, Canadian Pacific* at San Francisco Art Institute.
1892	SUMMER	Paints in White Mountains.
1893		Visits World's Columbian Exposition, Chicago, where he exhibits *California; A Scene near Los Gatos; The Driving of Last Spike; Muir Glacier, Alaska; The Grizzly Giant; Wawona; Big Tree Wawona;* and *Yosemite Valley from Inspiration Point.*
1894		Spends summer at Wawona. Donates painting of the Rio Grande to the Press Club.
1895	DECEMBER	Arrives in San Francisco, after seven months' absence, en route to Mount Baker.
1896	AUGUST	Suffers a stroke at studio.
	DECEMBER	Takes extended trip to Mexico and Southern California.
1903	MAY	Meets Theodore Roosevelt, whom he tours through studio at Wawona and presents a painting. Wife Charlotte dies on June 8.
1904–08		Health fails; spends summers in Wawona, winters in a cottage at Raymond. Requires constant care.
1908		Dies in Raymond on June 30.

INDEX

PHOTOGRAPHY CREDITS

Dan Babior: figs. 3, 5, 6, 78.

Cox Black and White Lab: fig. 79.

M. Lee Fatherree: pp. 2, 5, 100; figs. 15, 18, 21, 22, 23, 24, 27, 28, 41, 42, 43, 45, 53, 55, 59, 61, 62, 68, 74, 75, 81.

Robert MacKimmie: figs. 13, 20.

Melville McLean: fig. 3 (Gerdts).

William Nettles: cover; fig. 60.

Nikki Pahl: figs. 2, 70, 73.

Jeffrey Stewart: back cover; figs. 17, 25, 26, 29, 35, 36, 37, 47, 54, 82.

Robert Woolard: fig. 71.

Don Yee: figs. 19, 30, 67.

DIRECT FROM NATURE:
THE OIL SKETCHES OF THOMAS HILL

An exhibition organized by the Crocker Art Museum, Sacramento, California.

Crocker Art Museum, Sacramento, California
January 24–March 9, 1997

The Hyde Collection, Glens Falls, New York
April 12–May 18, 1997

The Currier Gallery of Art, Manchester, New Hampshire
September 26–December 1, 1997

LENDERS TO THE EXHIBITION

Candace McKee Ashmun
The Bancroft Library, University of California, Berkeley
Dr. and Mrs. Edward H. Boseker
George McNear Bowles
California Historical Society, San Francisco
Mary and Bruce Crawford
Crocker Art Museum, Sacramento
Fine Arts Museums of San Francisco
Garzoli Gallery, San Rafael, California
Gibson, Dunn & Crutcher, Los Angeles
The Gilcrease Museum, Tulsa, Oklahoma
Mrs. James R. Harvey
Leo and Florence Helzel
Stephen Hohener
Kenneth Householder
Herbert F. Johnson Museum of Art, Cornell University
William A. Karges
Kral Fine Arts, Oakland, California
Dr. and Mrs. Frank V. Kreske
Dr. Oscar and Trudy Lemer
New Hampshire Historical Society, Concord
Oakland Museum of California
Arthur J. Phelan, Jr.
Pittock Mansion Society, Portland, Oregon
Private collections
Mr. and Mrs. Garrett Plant Scales
Albert Shumate, M.D.
Mr. and Mrs. Charles W. Tuttle, Jr.
The Yosemite Museum, National Park Service

DIRECT FROM NATURE:
THE OIL SKETCHES OF THOMAS HILL

was designed by Sandy Bell, Springdale, Utah.
The text was set in Fairfield, designed by Rudolph Ruzicka in 1940.
The display type was set in Serlio.
The book was printed and bound in Hong Kong by Regal Printing
through Global Interprint, Inc.